DEATH
IN THE
MINES

DEATH
IN THE
MINES

DISASTERS AND RESCUES IN THE ANTHRACITE COAL FIELDS OF PENNSYLVANIA

J. STUART RICHARDS

THE
History
PRESS

Published by The History Press
Charleston, SC 29403
www.historypress.net

First published 2007

ISBN 978-1-5402-0446-2

Library of Congress Cataloging-in-Publication Data

Richards, J. Stuart, 1949-
Death in the mines : disasters and rescues in the anthracite coal fields
of Pennsylvania / J. Stuart Richards.
p. cm.
ISBN-13: 978-1-59629-211-6 (alk. paper)
1. Coal mine accidents--Pennsylvania--History--19th century. 2. Coal mine
accidents--Pennsylvania--History--20th century. 3. Coal mines and
mining--Pennsylvania--History--19th century. 4. Coal mines and
mining--Pennsylvania--History--20th century. 5. Coal
miners--Pennsylvania--History--19th century. 6. Coal
miners--Pennsylvania--History--20th century. 7. Mine rescue
work--Pennysylvania--History--19th century. 8. Mine rescue
work--Pennysylvania--History--20th century. I. Title.
TN805.P4R49 2006
363.11'962233409748--dc22
2006034633

For forty years I worked with pick and drill, down in the earth against my will, the coal king's slave but now it's past, thanks be to God I am free at last.
—*Epitaph on miner Condy Brisbin's tombstone, Hazelton, Pennsylvania*

CONTENTS

PREFACE

Anthracite coal mining and miners have always been a major part of my life. Members of my family have worked the anthracite mines of the middle and southern coal fields of eastern Pennsylvania since the early 1870s. Tragedy and death played a major part in many of their lives. My great-great-grandfather, Daniel Richards, came to this country as a miner from Wales and worked the mines of western Schuylkill County for twenty years. My great-grandfather, James Richards, and my grandfather, George (Gigi) Richards, started working in the mines as breaker boys at the early age of ten years. George worked in the anthracite mines for forty-three years until he collapsed from a weakened heart due to the effects of black lung and died at age fifty-three while working in a mine. His older brother, John, died in a fall of coal at the age of twenty-two years. My grandmother, Henrietta Withelder Richards, told me many times of the hard lives the women had while their husbands and brothers were away working in the mines. She related to me this story of her uncle, Henry Withelder, who on May 24, 1889, set off for work at the Otto Colliery near Branchdale, Pennsylvania. Henry was an experienced miner and this Friday would hopefully be just another day in the black pit. This day Henry would be working in the number forty-six breast of the East Red Ash gangway better known as the Primrose vein. The talk was that most of the men who worked this vein were afraid of working in the breasts because of the chance of a blower. A blower was a phenomenon that caused gas to seep out of cracks in the coal wall. If there was a spark or open flame the gas that escaped would explode, destroying everything in its path. The only way to survive was to throw oneself on the floor and keep one's face in the damp dirt to escape the flames. When the gas burned itself out, the men tried to escape as best they could. But there was another problem with a blower. The aftereffects of the explosion would cause a deadly gas known as afterdamp that, once inhaled, caused instant death.

Henry was working in number forty-six breast with a thirty-five-year-old miner named Anthony Zernheldt. On Saturday, May 25, 1889, the *Pottsville Miners Journal* ran a story called "Another Colliery Horror: Three Men Suffocated by Gas at the Otto Mine."

A terrible accident occurred at the Otto colliery between 12 and 1 o'clock yesterday afternoon by which three men, Anthony Zernheldt, Henry Withelder, and James Dolan, lost their lives painlessly and almost instantly. The accident occurred in what is known as the East Gangway or the Red Ash or "Neat" slope. Zernheldt and Withelder were working in the breast 46 and Dolan and a man named Mitchell were working in breast 47. Gas has been very troublesome at the Otto and the east side is worked entirely with safety lamps. These men were at work as usual yesterday, and heed every precaution to guard against the accident. It frequently happens however, in places where gas prevails in large quantities, that an outburst occurs when it is least expected. And only a swift retreat can save the miner from being caught by the suffocating element. In such instances a safety lamp saves them from a scorching death, but it is a rare chance that they can get out of the way quick enough to escape the breath of the pursuing fiend. This was the case with the unfortunate men yesterday. Zernheldt and Withelder were at work at the face of No. 46 breast, when they were startled by a sudden concussion below them. They knew what it meant, and headed for the heading, expecting to be able to get over into No. 47 and down through the manway before they were overcome. They gave an alarm and hurriedly crawled through the dim chamber for their lives. In the mean time Dolan and Mitchel who were at work at the face of breast 47 felt the concussion and began a hasty descent for their lives. Dolan took the left hand manway and Mitchell the right. By the merest chance Mitchell's life was saved. Breast 47 is about 40 yards up. Dolan hurried down the manway with all the speed possible. He got about half way down when he dropped. Zernheldt and Withelder followed, and were overcome at the same spot as Dolan as the three bodies were found lying in a heap. Mitchell got safely down from the fact that through the right hand manway the

PREFACE

air had an upward course, thus impeding the progress of the gas and neutralizing its effect.

Mitchell at once gave the alarm although the shock had been felt by a number of miners who were working nearby. All managed to get out safely. The next thing was to recover the bodies of the unfortunate men who were left behind, for there was no hope that they escaped death. District superintendent David Morris happened to be at the top of the slope when word of the terrible accident came up. He and inside Superintendent John Curran at once took measures to get the bodies out. On account of the gas, it would be impossible to reach them for several hours. Every device that could facilitate the process of ventilation was resorted to, but it was 9 o'clock before the workings were clear enough to allow any one to venture in. Finally when it was deemed safe to make the venture, and the fatal breast was reached, the men were found as above stated, lying together in a heap. There was not the slightest bruise upon any of the bodies, and the men, to all appearances were but sleeping. It was the sleep however, that knows no waking. The bodies were immediately hoisted to the top, where an ambulance was waiting to carry them to their respective homes. Zernheldt and Withelder reside in Newtown, and Dolan at Branchdale.

It is because of these family stories that I wanted to write a book, to share with people the many tragedies associated with coal mining and show the dangers the miners and boys and men who worked the anthracite coal fields of eastern Pennsylvania experienced and lived with on a daily basis and the toll it has taken on many families.

This book deals with the actual newspaper accounts of the accidents and the rescue attempts that occurred in the northern, southern and middle coal fields of eastern Pennsylvania. These dramatic stories serve as vivid reminders of the dangers that miners faced.

INTRODUCTION
ANTHRACITE COAL MINING

A nthracite mining is found in eight counties in the state of Pennsylvania: Carbon, Columbia, Dauphin, Lackawanna, Luzerne, Northumberland, Schuylkill and Sullivan. Over 90 percent of all the anthracite coal, or hard coal, mined in the United States is found in these eight counties of eastern Pennsylvania.

Anthracite coal reached its peak of production in the year 1917, when over one hundred million tons of coal were mined in Pennsylvania. The anthracite coal mining industry reached its peak in terms of employment and production in 1914 with close to 181,000 miners working in the collieries of Pennsylvania. In sharp contrast, in the year 2005, Pennsylvania anthracite coal mines employed just over 1,000 miners and mine workers.

Between 1870 and 2006 over 31,122 men and boys were killed in and about the anthracite coal mines of Pennsylvania. The highest number of men killed in accidents in the anthracite fields occurred in 1908 with a high of 708. During the years 1982, 1984, 1987 and 1992, not one mining death was recorded. Between the years 1847 and 1924 there were 96 accidents in which 5 or more men were killed in the anthracite coal mines for a total of 1,113 men killed in that time period.

Many nationalities worked in the anthracite coal mines of Pennsylvania. From the early days of anthracite mining English, Welsh and Germans composed the bulk of the mineworkers. An interesting aspect of the nationalities of the anthracite mine workers can be shown by the statistics

INTRODUCTION

The faces of labor, an excellent study of the anthracite coal miner. *Courtesy of the Historical Society of Schuylkill County.*

for the 1919–20 time period. There were 92,779 inside employees: 36,300 were classified as Americans; 19,641 as Poles; 10,041 as Lithuanians; 8,036 as Italians; 6,971 as Austrians; 5,890 as Russians; and 5,900 as Slavonians. Interestingly, of those classified as Americans at this time the majority was of Irish, Welsh and Scottish descent. The Irish, Welsh and Scottish were once the majority of the mineworkers but by 1920 they represented a little more than 7 percent of the total.

In the mines there are two classes of accidents that result in fatalities. First are the big disasters. In these disasters, large numbers of miners are killed or die from injuries sustained in the accidents. Second, there are minor accidents that occur almost every working day in the mines.

The inherent dangers that lay in wait in and around the anthracite colliery and coal mine are many. Gas explosions, mine fires, roof falls, underground flooding, breakers burning and collapsing, exploding boilers—all are part of the everyday dangers that the anthracite miner faced in the course of his dangerous work.

One of the dangers that a miner encounters in a working coal mine is the effect of gases given off by minerals and metals. The gas given off

most abundantly by coal is light carbureted hydrogen, known as marsh gas, because it is the product of vegetable decomposition during formation of the coal beds. It is commonly referred to by the miners as fire damp. It consists of four parts of hydrogen to one of carbon; it is half the weight of air and therefore rises to the roof of a mine. When it mixes with from four to twelve times its volume of atmospheric air it becomes violently explosive. A very dangerous aspect of this gas is that it sometimes does not escape the coal at a uniform rate, but will suddenly burst out in large volume. This action is called a blower. When this happens danger is imminent, and a disaster will shortly follow when a miner's naked flame lamp comes into contact with a large quantity of fire damp that has accumulated and is in an explosive state. The explosion that follows is tremendous. Men, mules, timbers, mine cars and anything lying around are blown about in a most terrific manner. Fire damp and an open flame have been the source of many mine disasters.

Another type of gas involved in mining accidents is black damp, a carbonic acid gas, containing two parts of oxygen to one of carbon (CO_2). It is heavier than air and therefore is found to be near the floor of the mine. A small percent of this gas may be breathed without immediate danger; it simply causes dullness and numbness of the body. If continued to be breathed, unconsciousness will occur and death will follow. The greatest danger of this

INTRODUCTION

Two miners are injured in an explosion deep in the mine. *Courtesy of the author.*

gas is found in abandoned workings where it will accumulate over a period of time. Another extremely dangerous gas, called white damp, consists of equal parts of oxygen and carbon. When present in a pure state it burns with a blue flame. It is tasteless and odorless, and its presence cannot be detected before it has done its deadly work. To breathe a small portion of this gas will immediately cause death. It is usually produced by burning timbers, smoldering gob fires or by a shaft fire, and was usually the cause of fatalities after an explosion had occurred. It is the most dreaded of all gases in a mine. An accumulation of black damp and white damp was the main cause of death in the famous Avondale Mine disaster in 1869.

All miners carried a safety lamp. The use of safety lamps was compulsory in any mine, especially the very gaseous ones. There were many types of safety lamps employed in the mines, including Davy, Wolf and Kohler, to name a few. All the safety lamps worked on the same principle. The flame is protected from the gas by a thin gauze of very fine mesh so that the flame will not ignite the gas that is present outside the lamp. The principle is that the heat from the flame will attract the air. If flammable gas (fire damp) is present the flame will burn brighter; if bad air (black damp CO_2) is evident the flame will go out due to lack of oxygen.

Explosions and fires can occur in mines that are well ventilated, which precludes the initial evidence that mining accidents occured only in mines that weren't properly ventilated. Pillars of coal from old worked out sections

ANTHRACITE COAL MINING

A miner is laid out on a hard wooden bed in this underground hospital. Note the whitewashed timbers and the cabinet with medical supplies. *Courtesy of the author.*

of mines weakened by the heavy pressure exerted downward on them can suddenly collapse, which can cause a chain reaction where a large area of overhead roof will suddenly collapse. This collapse causes an enormous amount of dust to accumulate and any spark will cause an explosion.

Water is another ever-present danger in a working mine. Floods may occur in low-lying abandoned workings, or may occur when working underground near a river or stream. Heavy rain can also cause the possibility of a sudden in-rush of water. One of the most feared dangers in a working mine of this time period was that of a "mine squeeze," the sudden upheaval of the floor or sagging of the roof, crushing the timbers and coal pillars.

The colliery whistle, located at the boiler house, sounded the alarm when a disaster occurred. When the whistle sounded a twenty-second blast, it indicated that a problem had occurred in the colliery. Then, by word of mouth or a courier running to a telegraph office, help was summoned. The news of the accident spread like wildfire and caused great excitement in the surrounding mining villages, known in local slang as patch towns. Most of the patch town residents had relatives working in the mines. Upon hearing the whistle, friends and family members immediately rushed to the colliery or mine entrance and waited. The anxiety was terrible. Minutes turned to hours for the waiting families. When word finally reached the surface, the mothers and wives would rush forward to the entrance. As one reporter recorded, "It was heartrending to witness the tears and hear the cries of distress."

INTRODUCTION

The colliery ambulance known as the Black Maria. *Courtesy of the Historical Society of Schuylkill County.*

The work of rescuing the survivors, if there were any, was hard and dangerous. Many miners were killed while trying to rescue men trapped deep underground. The rescue efforts would continue for days while authorities tried to figure out what exactly happened underground. Rumors raged throughout the area as to who survived, who was injured or what caused the disaster. Anger was always aimed at the company authorities for covering up the information or not releasing enough information. After the bodies of the victims were retrieved, they were brought to the surface, where they were sometimes placed in a black wagon that was called the "Black Maria pulled by two horses." This wagon served two purposes. The first purpose was to serve as an ambulance to take a critically injured miner to his home or the hospital. The second purpose was to serve as a hearse to bring the dead miner from the mine to his home. All mining families dreaded the appearance of the Black Maria coming to their homes. This scene was repeated hundreds of times throughout the anthracite coalfields of eastern Pennsylvania.

1.

FIRE IN THE MINES

AVONDALE
"AN APPALLING ACCIDENT"
AVONDALE, PENNSYLVANIA
SEPTEMBER 6, 1869

On September 6, 1869, at Avondale, Pennsylvania, a large wooden coal breaker that covered the mouth of the shaft, which was the only entrance and exit into the mine, caught fire and trapped and asphyxiated 108 men and boys who were at work deep in the mine. The fire was caused by the use of an open-flame furnace deep in the mine near the shaft. It was used to create an updraft of heat, which in turn caused a downdraft of fresh air. This disaster brought widespread attention to the appalling conditions of the coal mines of this country.

On March 3, 1870, the legislature of Pennsylvania passed the first law in the United States for the regulation and inspection of coal mines. This law applied only to the anthracite coal mines. The law stated that all accidents would be investigated and that an accurate and systematic mapping of mine workings would be instituted. At least two openings would be used in a mine, and both would be equipped so that they could be used as an escape passage during any type of accident. There was also a provision for a certain quantity of air for each person employed in the mine.

The Avondale disaster was reported on September 11, 1869, in the *Pottsville Miners Journal*.

AVONDALE, "AN APPALLING ACCIDENT"

Miners stand at the entrance to a drift in this nineteenth-century photograph. Note the early style coal car. *Courtesy of the Historical Society of Schuylkill County.*

On Monday last, the engine house, breakers, attached to the Avondale colliery situated at Plymouth, in Luzerne County, and about twenty miles from Scranton, was totally destroyed by fire. The most appalling fact of the accident was, that through the destruction of buildings was brought about one of the most terrible and lamentable mining catastrophes that has ever occurred in this state. At the time of the fire—which appears to have been caused by the flames from a ventilating furnace at the bottom of the shaft setting fire to the woodwork dividing the shaft, and thereby communicating it to the buildings immediately above it—about one hundred and fifteen or twenty persons, as near as we can learn, were working in the mines. Having no means of egress other than through the shaft, and all communication being cut off, before aid could reach them all perished by suffocation. At first the wildest rumors prevailed in reference to the loss of life, the estimate being that over two hundred miners had perished; but the latest accounts state that all the bodies have been recovered, and number 108. There are 50 widows and 109 orphans made by this disaster.

Many of the scenes and incidents are of a most touching and soul harrowing description. On Wednesday morning, the first door of the gangway was broken in, and sixty bodies were found there. Their situation was awful; fathers lay stiff in death with arms about their sons. Some were kneeling as though in prayer, strong men were hand in hand with their fellows. The pickaxes and shovels, which they had used in making an embankment to prevent the entrance of foul air, lay on one side. It seemed, then, that they had fled a few steps, when in an agony they fell in one another's arms, suffocated by the deadly smoke. In another chamber every man was without a shirt. They had stripped themselves of clothes to use them in filling up crevices and crannies. One man had pushed a part of his garment into an aperture, when a gust of the gas rushed through and strangled him to death. Wagon loads of coffins line the road, and litters filled with sheeted dead pass along the line every few minutes.

A correspondent says that the scene at night was a strange one. For many miles up and down this beautiful valley the glare of thousand lights were seen. The vast quantities of burning coal at the breaker were covered with sheets of colored flame. Great brawny men worked silently and constantly, and often in tears. At intervals a mothers wail came in on the night air, as it did years ago when death once reigned in the valley of the Wyoming. Long lines of men guarded the hoisting rope on either side, while those at their posts attended to the duties assigned them.

Every fifteen minutes a dead body was hoisted. The volunteer miners who went down to rescue the bodies were in many cases overcome by the noxious gases. In almost every instance it was necessary to apply restoratives, so great was the exhaustion. The bodies all, as a general thing, presented a horrible appearance; yet they did not seem to give much expression of pain in the faces of some, but rather a look of resignation to an inevitable fate, which gives to some a calm and undisturbed appearance.

Much sympathy is felt and expressed for the victims of the Avondale catastrophe and steps are now being taken to raise a fund to procure each of the families a homestead. It is to be hoped sincerely, that the effort will be successful.

We trust that Schuylkill county will not be behind in the good work of subscribing for the relief of the Avondale sufferers. We would suggest the calling of a public meeting or some other mode for the purpose of giving effect to the philanthropic work. In the meantime, those wishing to contribute to the relief of the widows and orphans at Avondale, can forward the same to W.S. Wilson First National Bank, Plymouth. It has been suggested that collections for the purpose be taken up in the churches of this borough, to-morrow. We hope that it will be done, not only in the borough but throughout the county.

Avondale, "An Appalling Accident"

An interesting editorial followed the first day's stories concerning the accident. It dealt with the need for some kind of legislature for the safe operation of the mines.

> The Avondale disaster has opened the eyes of the people of some of our neighboring counties to the want of adequate legislation for the better protection of the life of miners in their respective localities. Our mind has long been impressed with this idea, and about eight years ago, was assisted in the preparation of a bill having for its object the supplying of this want. That bill, drawn up with much careful solicitude and thoughtful consideration, and which we think was well calculated to cover the desired grounds, was forwarded to Harrisburg but, through a combination of circumstances, never acted upon. Last winter, through the instrumentality of our members, a bill of a similar character, defective in some points, but in the main satisfactory, was acted upon and passed. This bill, so far as this county is concerned, makes some wise provisions for the better ventilation of the mines, and protects, to a certain degree, the lives of the miners. By it we have an inspector of the mines whose duty it is, among others, to see that the mines are properly ventilated, and to see that the workmen have the proper means of application for egress in case of accidents. Now, had this law been extended to Luzerne county, and placed in practical operation, through competent and skilled inspector, the community might have been spared the harrowing recital of the recent horrible disaster.
>
> Now the best thing the people of our sister counties can do in this matter, is to have a bill framed in such a way as to meet the present exigencies, or have the provisions of the Schuylkill county act extended to them, and insist on their legislation having it done.

In the days following the accident the *Miners Journal* published articles concerning the testimony of some of the witnesses in the accident and some of the speculation that would follow a major accident.

> The *Scranton Republican* seems to create the impression that the Avondale colliery was set on fire, from the testimony taken. We of course are not sufficiently acquainted with the position of the colliery and the furnace to express an opinion on the subject. But we see nothing in the testimony as far as we have read it, to confirm

such an opinion. If combustibles had been placed in the air shaft, it must have been done at night, as the fire in the furnace was made with wood at 6 o'clock, which would create a great blaze in the up current, it would have occurred very shortly after, but the testimony says it did not occur until 10 o'clock—four hours after. Making up a fire with wood in a furnace to give draft to the up current of air, without putting on coal almost immediately to check the flame, would carry it a great distance from the furnace.

One of the witnesses testified before the Coroner's Jury that he first saw the fire at the head of the flue about the mouth of the shaft, and he supposed it was caused by the NEW FIREMAN WHO DID NOT KNOW EXACTLY HOW TO BUILD THE FIRE. The lower portion of the wooden flue was, of course damp, as the fire had been out from Saturday to Monday, and the upper end and dryer portion of the brattice work would be more likely to take fire from the flame extending upward, and afterward was gradually fanned in a flame.

There is so much feeling on this subject, between the men and also the company, that all such testimony must be sifted very closely, and but little credit attached unless their [sic] is positive evidence. The *Republican* during the suspension made a number of false charges against those who were in favor of the basis, and also against the people of Schuylkill county.

During the investigation much controversy arose concerning the cause of the fire. The Miners Union denied all charges of the Delaware, Lackawanna and Western Railroad Company that the fire was intentionally set. The miners published their own response to these charges. The following article was published in the *Pottsville Miners Journal* of September 18, 1869.

The Miners Union desire that the following statement on their part be given to the public:

The dispatches which are being constantly transmitted from Scranton in relation to the Avondale disaster are in many instances entirely unfounded in fact. That the fire which occurred at the mines was the work of an incendiary no one believes. It is one of the subterfuges resorted to by the Delaware and Lackawanna and Western Railroad Company to turn the mind of the public from the real responsibility resting upon the company. The reporters who furnish principally the particulars taken before the jury of inquest

Avondale, "An Appalling Accident"

A good view of an underground mule stable. The mules were well taken care of in the mine. *Courtesy of the author.*

on Saturday last have, in many instances, suppressed the testimony material to the miners, and published that favorable to the company. The object can only be conjectured. The company is powerful; the miners are weak. Simple justice is the demand of many citizens.

The final out come to this tragic disaster was that the ventilating furnace set fire to the woodwork in the main shaft. The fire was discovered in the morning by the stable boss. He had just entered the mine with hay for the mules. Within minutes the flames rose in the up draft and reached the breaker above setting it and the engine house on fire. The hoisting engineer had to flee the engine house stranding all those below who died from the effects of the mine gasses and smoke. After the fire was extinguished, a dog enclosed in a box with a lighted lantern placed on top, was lowered into the depths of the mine to test the quality of the air. The dog survived but the lamp was blown out. This indicated the presence of black damp, or carbonic acid gas. Thinking that some of the miners might still be alive, two brave Welshmen volunteered to be lowered into the mine, Thomas W. Williams of Plymouth and David Jones, of Grand Tunnel. When they reached the bottom of the shaft, both men began digging, but were soon overcome by the dreaded gas and suffocated. Waiting until the early morning hours of Tuesday, the rescuers finally reached the place where some of the miners had built a barricade in the hopes of saving themselves from the smoke and gas. Beyond the barricade lay the bodies of over sixty miners huddled together. The final death toll was 110 men.

On September 9, 1869, the *New York Tribune* ran a list of those killed in the Avondale Catastrophe:
Steele, Palmer, stable boss, Plymouth

Two Hundred Miners Suffocated in the Avondale Colliery Fire
The list of the dead miners, labors and driver boys.

Slocum, Dennis, driver, Plymouth
Bowen, John, formerly of Providence.
   He leaves a wife and one child.
Powell, William, wife and seven
   children in the old country; one
   daughter lives in Plymouth and one
   son was in the mine.
Williams, Wm., Hyde Park, 14 yrs of age,
   who had only worked there one day.
Evans, Matthew, of Steuben Colliery.
Evans, William, a brother of Matthew,
   of Steuben Colliery.
Mosier, Matthew, Plymouth, leaves wife
   and child.
Clark, John, Jersey Hill, Plymouth,
   leaves wife and seven children.
Evans, Wm. J., Turkey Hill, leaves wife
   and two or three children.
Stackhouse, George, Avondale, driver,
   aged 17, unmarried.
Jones, Edwin Hanover, leaves a wife.
Conklin, Peter, of Plymouth, has a wife
   and three children in England.
Watkins, Morgan, Plymouth,
   unmarried.
Frothingham, Andrew, Avondale, leaves
   a wife.

Allen, Wm., Hanover, leaves a wife,
   soon to be a mother.
Jones, T.E., formerly of Providence,
   leaves a wife and widowed mother.
Johnson, Peter, Plymouth, unmarried.
Hughes, Evan, inside boss, Plymouth,
   brother of Benjamin Hughes, of
   Scranton, leaves a wife and three
   children.
Bowen, Wm., Avondale, wife and one
   child.
Powel, James L., son of Wm. Powell,
   unmarried.
Hughes, Thomas, Welch Hill, Plymouth.
Reece, Wm., Cold Street, Plymouth, wife
   in the old country. His step-father
   and brother were both in the mine.
Porfit, Wm., Plymouth, wife and two
   children.
Williams, W.N., Plymouth, wife and
   three children.
Lewis, Wm., Plymouth, wife and child.
Hughes, John, Plymouth, wife and child.
Morris, Thos., Plymouth, wife and four
   children.
Bryant, Elijah, Avondale, wife and child.
Roberts, Thomas, Plymouth, single.

Sink, Wm., Avondale, single.

Jones, Daniel, Plymouth, family in England.

Thomas, David, cousin to the two who were brought out, Plymouth, unmarried, parents in the old country.

Givens, David, aged 17, car driver, parents at Kingston.

Rees, Evan, Plymouth, wife and child in Wales.

Edwards, E.W., Plymouth, wife and child.

Morris, Henry, Plymouth.

Williams, W.T., 39, Hyde Park, wife and child.

Reese, D.S., Plymouth, wife and four children. Two sons in mine.

Woolley, Richard, Plymouth, single.

Davis, John R., formerly of Pittston.

James, David, Kingston, wife and child.

Evans, Williams, son of Wm. E. Evans, in mine, has a mother and a sister.

Williams, Wm. (shoemaker), Plymouth, aged about 40, wife.

Owens, Richard, Avondale, wife.

Hatton, Willie, about 10 yrs old, Plymouth.

Evans, Wm., Avondale, uncle of Wm. E. Davis, aged 51, driver boss, wife.

Powell, James, Plymouth, single.

Hatton, Thos., father of the boy Willie, Plymouth, wife and two living children.

Owen, Edward, Baltimore, MD, wife and family in Baltimore.

Burtch, John and John, Jr., age about 12, Plymouth, formerly of Providence, wife and three children.

Jenkins, John, inside boss.

Evans, Wm. R., second son of Mr. Evans brought out.

Wood, Daniel, Plymouth, wife and two children.

Moses, Wm., Plymouth, age about 14.

Reese, David Jr., Plymouth, father and brother brought out dead.

Roberts, Griffith, Plymouth, lived with parents.

Man, named unknown.

Morris, Joseph, Plymouth, wife.

Ruth, John, Hanover, wife and child.

McGurick, Patrick, wife and three children.

Smith, Henry, Avondale, wife and three children.

Howells, Shem, Welch Hill, Plymouth, wife and four small children.

Davis, Thos., Plymouth, family in Wales.

Dowdle, Wm., Avondale, single.

Roberty, John, single.

Ryan, Thos., Avondale, mother at Grand Tunnel.

Gilroy, Hugh, son of Patrick Gilroy who recognized him, as did also a brother, married and one child, but did not live with wife.

Maher, John, Avondale, 40, wife and one child.

Morgan, Wm. T., Plymouth.

Murray, James, Avondale, wife and two children.

Daly, Michael, wife and four children.

Pryor, D.P., Avondale, wife and two children.

Burke, Patrick, Plymouth, has a sister in Scranton.

DEATH IN THE MINES

Williams, James, Plymouth, wife and two children.

Evans, John D., Plymouth, wife and five children.

Harding, Wm., Plymouth, came from Hyde Park, wife.

Morgan, Samuel R., Plymouth, wife and four children, three of whom boys, were in the mine and brought out dead.

Wildrich, Wm., Hanover, wife and four children.

Lunday, Reese, of Turkey Hill, wife and three children.

Lewellyn, Thos., Plymouth, single.

Lewellyn, Reese, brother to preceding, single.

Davis, Wm., Plymouth, wife and children in the old country.

Thomas, John, Plymouth, wife and one child.

Davis, John, Plymouth, formerly of Pittston.

Williams, William T., Plymouth, wife and four children.

Jones, Wm. D., wife and four children in Aberdare, South Wales.

Guyter, Darrius, Avondale, wife and three children.

Rees, Wm., wife and children in Neath, South Wales.

Spick, Wm., Plymouth, wife and one child.

Harris, John, Avondale, wife and children.

Jones, Thomas, Plymouth, wife and children. Buried one child last Sunday.

Phillips, Thos., Plymouth, single.

Davis, Lewis, boarded with Evan Hughes, single man.

Fear, Charles, Plymouth.

Thomas, John, Plymouth, aged 17.

Johnson, Dave, Plymouth, wife and one child.

Mallon, James, Plymouth, single.

Haskins, James, Plymouth, wife and three children.

Jones, Wm. D., wife in Merthyr Tydvil.

Taylor, Edward, Avondale, single.

Jones, Roland, Turkey Hill, wife and two children.

Allibach, Addison, Plymouth, wife and three children.

Edwards, Daniel, Avondale, wife and one child.

Powell, John, Avondale, formerly of Tenn., wife and two children.

LUKE FIDLER COLLIERY
"A FRIGHTFUL DISASTER"
SHAMOKIN, PENNSYLVANIA
OCTOBER 10, 1894

As a carpenter worked to repair the timbers in the Luke Fidler shaft, a miner's lamp on his head accidentally caught some dry brattice and timbers on fire. The fire spread rapidly and seventy miners and carpenters rushed for safety through a shaft under construction and were hoisted to the surface. Unfortunately, five other men and boys were trapped in the mine.

This record is from the *Pottsville Miners Journal*, October 10, 1894.

Shamokin—Oct. 9, One of the most disastrous mine fires in the history of the anthracite fields of Pennsylvania started at the Luke Fidler colliery last evening, and besides the hundreds of thousand of dollars worth of damage done at the Luke Fidler and Gimlet and Hickory Swamp workings, five and possibly eight homes were rendered desolate by the awful work of the flames. Those known to be dead are as follows: Irvin Buffington, carpenter; Stanney Booerer, driver boy; George Brown, miner; George Browns, laborer; name unknown; Joe Viskeyski, laborer; name unknown.

Last evening Irvin Buffington, in company with a number of other carpenters, was working about half way down the shaft caulking up holes in the side of the brattice which connects the shaft with the air passage. It is the rule when doing this work for the men to use lanterns,

DEATH IN THE MINES

The Luke Fidler Colliery, Shamokin, Pennsylvania. Scene of a frightful fire on October 10, 1894. *Harold C. Koons collection, John Pritiskutch Reproduction.*

but in this case the rule was discarded and naked lamps substituted. Detecting a leak Buffington placed his lamp to the draft and the flame immediately caught the boards, which were saturated with oil, and was taken into the air chamber. Realizing the awful consequences of his act, the man at once started for the bottom of the shaft to notify the workmen employed there of their danger and to get a few of his belongings, among which was a pair of shoes kept in an old chest. Getting these Buffington started up the shaft again, and succeeded in reaching the tunnel leading to the top. By this time he was nearly exhausted, but staggered on and succeeded in traveling two hundred yards, but when within thirty feet of the door of the passage way leading to the open air he was overcome by the smoke and fell. He again tried to reach the haven of safety, but his efforts were of no avail, and his remains were found lying at the above mentioned place at 5 o'clock this morning. Death had been caused by suffocation.

David Muir, one of the persons warned by the carpenter, took the same method of getting out, and was near Buffington when he fell, but being almost dead from exhaustion, and nearly suffocated by the intense smoke which filled the tunnel, was obliged to let him remain, but succeeded in dragging himself inside the traveling way door, and after gathering strength was able to reach open air.

Luke Fidler Colliery, "A Frightful Disaster"

Michael Golden, one of the inside officials, was at the bottom of the shaft when the alarm was given, and at once notified the men working in No. 3 slope, while Johnny Dunmore performed a like duty for those employed in No. 2 slope. Golden knew the workings from one end to the other and told the men of an opening by which it was possible to reach the new shaft which had but recently been completed. Leading the way for the seventy men who are employed in this part of the mine, the boss made for the passage, which was safely reached, although it was nearly filled with smoke. The iron bucket used to hoist the men holds about six persons. This was quickly filled and in response to the frantic signal given by those below, Engineer Jack Ratigan began to hoist. Nearly ten trips had been made when it was discovered that a number were missing, and their comrades thought that they surely had met death. Among those who tried to reach the top by the way of the old shaft were David Edmonds and Harry Evans. They had succeeded in getting up about half way when the smoke became too thick and they were forced back. The traveling way to the east shaft was then tried with better results, although the smoke was very strong. When nearly halfway to safety Evans, who is but a boy, gave out, and to save his young comrade from a certain death, Edmunds picked him up and succeeded in reaching open air. Two miners, whose names could not be obtained, seeing that escape through the old shaft was impossible, and that their retreat in the direction of the new one was covered with smoke, grouped their way back further, and succeeded in reaching safely an opening which came out on the top of the mountain.

Several men ran towards the Coal Run workings and made their escape in that direction. Among the last to escape from No. 3 slope was a Hungarian, who excitedly told the men at the bottom of the new shaft waiting to be hoisted, in his broken English, that there were three fellows overcome by smoke while getting out of the working, and they were nearly dead.

Somebody suggested that a party be formed to go back and rescue them, but it was clearly seen that the course would be suicidal, so it was abandoned, and the sufferers left to their fate.

The fire had been scarcely started a minute before up through the air passage shot a sheet of flame twenty feet high. It was scarcely three minutes before the fan house was one mass of blackened cinders. The signal of fire was at once given, and in an incredibly short time people poured from every direction. They came over the hill from Springfield and up the railroad from Shamokin.

The Shamokin fire department was quick to respond, and soon the Independence, Friendship and Liberty Hose Companies were on the ground. Several of these were told that their services weren't needed and at once returned to their houses. However, it was but a short time later that word was dispatched to them to come again and bring the steamer with them. This was done, and from 9 o'clock last evening until the present time the brave fire laddies have done all in their power to quench the flames.

Superintendent Williams and Mine Inspector Brennan were quickly at the colliery, and soon had order out of chaos. Rescuing parties were formed, but before they could reach places where men were known to have worked they were driven back by the smoke.

This morning another consultation was held and the advisability of attempting to rescue the enclosed men discussed. Mine Inspector Brennan was almost wild with the desire to get them out, but was decided the effort was worse than useless, as it was almost certain to result in the death of some of the rescuing party.

There are altogether 1,000 men employed at the Luke Fidler, and these, with those who are thrown out of work at the other two collieries, will make 2,000 who will have to undergo enforced idleness of many months. The latest plan of the officials to quench the burning inside is by pumping all the available water into the mines and drowning it out. This however, will take months to accomplish, and it is safe to say that this valuable coal operation is practically ruined, entailing a loss to its owners of several hundred thousand dollars. It was one of the few collieries which gave steady employment to its employees, and the loss to the workingman of Shamokin will be severely felt.

At 9:25 o'clock tonight no news had been received regarding the fate of George Brown and the three entombed Polish miners. It is certain that all are dead. A rumor is current this evening that two Hungarians are unaccounted for, but the officials state positively that there are only four men left in the mine. The mine is still burning and will have to be flooded. The loss at Luke Fidler will amount to $700,000.

Luke Fidler Colliery, "A Frightful Disaster"

On October 11, 1894, the *Pottsville Miners Journal* reported that the recovery of the bodies might never take place. The fire was still burning and the mine workings were miles in length. To extinguish the fire might take months.

A terrific explosion occurred in the ill fated Luke Fidler mine this afternoon, the shock of which was felt a mile distant. It was caused by the accumulation of gas and sulphur. The extent of the damage done cannot be ascertained, as no one has been able to go near the workings, where the fire of yesterday is still raging fiercely.

It has been decided by the officials of the Mineral Mining Company that there is only one way to extinguish the fire, and that is by flooding the mines. In order to do this arrangements are being made to turn the water from Coal Run stream into the workings. Although strenuous efforts were made, it was impossible for any persons to get near the workings on account of gas, so all endeavors to take the remains of the supposed dead from the burning furnace were futile, and the hope was finally abandoned.

The No. I shaft in which the fire is raging most fiercely, is now being filled with water and dirt, and the intention of the company is to make it solid, in order to smother the flame if possible. The connection between the burning mine and the Colbert Colliery is being bratticed off, so as to allow the Union Coal Company's operation to commence work. The Colbert started up this morning, and by keeping the Fidler fans idle it is altogether probable the fire will not reach that colliery.

Just how many months before the fire can be extinguished it was impossible for officials today to give an idea. But it will be a long time, as the workings extended into many directions and are miles in length. As the flames eat out the timbers the top of tunnels and gangways will fall, blocking up the passage way of the water, making the conditions such that the fire will have to die out, in some portions of the mine of its own accord.

Everything will be done by the company to mend matters as soon as possible. There was a rumor current last evening that the entire Luke Fidler would be abandoned, but the coal mined at the colliery is of too good quality to justify such a proceeding. Although the anthracite taken from the working now on fire had formed a market especially for its self, endeavors will be made to fill all orders from the Cameron colliery. The coal mined at this colliery is slightly softer, and up to some time ago was a little dirty. This can now be avoided by the use of a new jig house; which went into operation on Monday for the first time.

It is now positive that there are only four men in the workings, as all the rest have been accounted for. The family of George Brown can scarcely be made to believe that he is one of the unfortunates, but there seems to be no other explanation of his absence. It is altogether likely that the remains of the poor fellow will never be found, as the fire in all probability has long ere reached the spot were they are supposed to be.

The heroic action of Michael Golden and Johnny Dunmore in going back to the No. 2 and No. 3 slopes to warn their comrades of the danger, has received much comment, and their work alone may the credit be given that the dead men do not now number nearly fifty instead of five. The number of brave deeds done during the frightful catastrophe of Monday will doubtless never be known, and it is very likely that some of those whose remains are by this time cremated met death in a vain effort to save the life of a fellow workman.

This afternoon Mine Inspector Brennan headed a rescuing party through a mine breach in the mountain to look for that last time for the entombed miners, but the expedition failed on account of the dense smoke and the bad air.

The mine inspector's report put the total blame for the fire on the carpenter Irvin Buffington. He stated that the shaft is operated by boreholes from the surface. The construction of it is such that the steam pipes are very close to the air compartment, thus making the brattice and timber in one end of the shaft very dry. For this reason only lanterns were used while making repairs, and for fear of fire even smoking was prohibited. Notwithstanding these rules, Buffington, in direct violation of orders, used a naked light and foolishly placed it against the brattice to look for a leak, thinking to discover it by having the flame draw up through the opening. In doing this he set the brattice on fire, and everything was dry as tinder. There was no possibility of extinguishing it. Buffington paid the penalty of this violation of orders with his life.

PANCOAST COLLIERY
"LIKE RATS IN A TRAP"
THROOP, PENNSYLVANIA
APRIL 7, 1911

Nearly one mile from the foot of the shaft of the Pancoast mine, three hundred men were at work when a fire started. The source of the fire was the engine house, which is built on the bottom of the six-hundred-foot shaft. Mine law stated, after the great Avondale disaster, that there must be two openings in a mine for safety reasons. But what went wrong in this mine? Why were seventy-two men killed? The company claimed all safety concerns were met and the men had sufficient time to get to safety. Following is the tragic story of the disaster and the rescue attempt from the *Pottsville Daily Republican* on April 7, 1911.

Scranton, Pa.—Fifty to seventy men employed in the Pancoast mine of the Scranton Coal Co. at Throop are entombed in the inner workings with all chance of escape cut off.

Fire is raging along the entire vein owing to an engine house having been set, shortly before 11 o'clock this morning. The mine is equipped with two openings but the location of the burning engine room is such as to have cut off escape by these routes.

The fire is in the workings, 750 feet below the surface. Officials, scores of workmen, volunteer firemen and the Throop fire department are working to get to the men supposed to be in one part of the mine.

DEATH IN THE MINES

This a view of what most collieries in the anthracite region looked like, including the head frame over the shaft or slope, the engine hose and the pump house. *Courtesy of the author.*

The fire is reported to have started in an engine room at the head of the slope, from an unknown cause.

Three hundred men were in the mines when the alarm was given and, on account of the great excitement, it is impossible to learn just how many managed to get out. Unless the men thought to be trapped are soon reached, it is feared they will soon die, if they have not already been smothered by smoke.

At 1:30 o'clock this afternoon it was explained that it was impossible to reach the men for some time, owing to the smoke and the great distance they are below the surface. At that hour it was admitted by one of the officials that there was a fire in the mine, but the official was unwilling to even venture an opinion as to how many men were trapped. The news of the fire spread rapidly and hundreds flocked to the mouth of the shaft. Women were frantic and tore their hair and clothing in their despair, many of them having to be taken from the scene.

Under the mining law of Pennsylvania a second opening in the mines is required, as it is believed that the mine workers would all be able to get out of one of the two exits. An investigation showed, however that the fire is located as to cut off escape from both openings.

When the seriousness of the situation dawned upon the mining officials, the rescue station at Wilkes Barre was immediately notified and the Delaware, Lackawanna & Western Railroad

Emergency car was sent to Throop with the crew. They carried with them oxygen helmets and other equipment to fight the fire.

Throop is about four miles north of this city and the Pancoast mine is in the town. It is said that a majority of the men in the mine are foreign born laborers.

At 2:30 P.M. the fire in the mine is still burning. The mine officials cling to the hope that the entombed men will be rescued alive, but those around the mine opening take a gloomy view and say the chance of recovery is very slight.

The fire is in a slope, 750 feet from the surface. It started at 9:30 o'clock this morning in an engine house and communicated to coal cars standing in the roadway. Water has been carried in a line of hose to the locality of the fire, but the heat is so intense and the smoke so dense that the rescuers are having the greatest difficulty in fighting the flames.

There were three hundred men in the mine when the fire broke out, and all escaped except the party who were in the blind gangway beyond the engine house and who got out reported the imprisonment of the party of their fellow workmen.

3:15 P.M. Three helmets and oxygen tanks were sent to the slope. It is the intention to send three rescuers protected by these appliances past the fire to the gangway, where the imprisoned men are supposed to be. Nothing will be known of the fate of the 40 men until these rescuers return, which may be in the course of a half an hour.

The fire fighters in the volunteer rescue corps at the mine aided by the helmet men of the government and the Delaware, Lackawanna and Western Coal Company rescue cars reached the first bodies at 6 o'clock last night, but the work of bringing out the dead proceeded slowly owing to the intense heat of the vein where they met their death and the quantities of smoke that it was impossible to get out of the working until hours after the fire had been extinguished. Not until the erection of brattices made it possible to get a change of the air currents did the rescue men clear the vein of the smoke and make it possible to bring out the dead without the extreme danger to themselves which existed in their first attempts to reach them.

At midnight twenty-one bodies had been brought to the foot of the shaft, and at four o'clock this morning 36 bodies were on the surface, all with the exception of five, being identified. Since then the dead have been sent up the shaft steadily and at eight o'clock the total had reached fifty-six.

DEATH IN THE MINES

So many homes are stricken that practically half the little mining town is in mourning, and so many wage earners are gone that dire distress is expected to follow in the many homes from which they have been taken. Arrangements are being made to care for the unfortunates.

Now will follow the investigation to ascertain who is responsible for the death of the victims. The mining law provides that there shall be two exits from a vein. In this case there was only one and at the mouth of it the fire raged, preventing the escape of the men. It is also said that the engine house where the fire started and which is at the top of the slope leading to the vein where the men worked caught fire early in the morning but that the officials kept on hoisting coal for some time by means of another engine and that the fire was not thought to be serious. A thorough investigation will be made by direction of the Chief James R. Roderick, of the state mining department.

At 10 o'clock this morning sixteen more bodies had been found bringing the total up to seventy, considerably more than the officials thought were in the workings. Twelve of the sixteen bodies had been brought to the surface and four more are awaiting at the foot of the shaft. The officials admit reluctantly that there may still be as many as ten bodies in the colliery.

Rescuers are still bringing out the bodies by ones and twos and there is a large section of the vein which has not yet been explored. Progress is slow owing to the smoke hampering in the work of the rescuers. Among the dead are ten small boys who were driving mules and attending doors.

After a long night of labor in the blackened depths of the Pancoast mine at Throop, the bodies of fifty-six of the victims had been brought to the surface by 8 o'clock this morning and the mine officials believe that there are still ten to fifteen in the far corners of the China vein, where the unfortunates were caught by the fire which broke out yesterday, like rats in a trap.

The work of the rescuers was suddenly stopped at 6 o'clock this morning by the fire breaking out and it is now raging fiercely with the fire fighting corps striving valiantly to overcome it.

Dr. J.A. Holmes, chief of the government mine rescue corps and J.W. Roberts, superintendent of the corps from Washington D.C., reached the scene this morning on a special train and have taken charge of the rescue work aided by the mine officials and many experienced mining men who have volunteered their services. They say that they expect the fire to be quenched in a few hours and that the remainder of the bodies will be brought out during the day.

Pancoast Colliery "Like Rats in a Trap"

Dr. Holmes will not make any statement as yet regarding the failure of the fire helmets to work as expected last night and causing the death of rescue foreman Joseph E. Evans and the prostration and narrow escape from death of Chief Engineer Charles Enzian, of Wilkes Barre.

It is believed by mining men that these rescue corps officials in the effort to make a great record on the first attempt at rescue work, pushed far into the fiery workings and that the intense heat caused the oxygen in their helmets and the oxygen in their tanks to expand. Both were overcome and Evans died four hours after being brought out while Enzian is still weak, but out of danger.

Forty-four of the dead have been identified. Many of the victims being foreigners, their identification is difficult. Heading the list of victims comes Joseph Evans 35 years old, living in West Scranton, who was foreman of the U.S. Rescue car which was hurried to the mine from its Wilkes Barre station. Evans was leading a rescue party into the smoke laden, black damp filled mine. Dr. J. Holmes said: "There are martyrs in every cause. Ours has Evans for its first."

The English speaking miners of the tragedy are:

Walter Knight, mine foreman, married, five children; Isaac Dawes, fire boss, married, three children; Joseph Perry, miner, married, one child. He was a Scranton City Councilman. John May, company hand, married, three children; John Gregson, company hand, single; Edward Hart, foot tender, married, six children; James Wallace, company hand, married, six children; Thomas MacWaters, miner, married, five children; Michael Gall, miner, married; Harry Rothwell, miner, married; Lawerence Ritz, doorman, married, one son.

Others among the victims are John Stroyak, who is survived by five children; two sons, Stephen and John, one a door boy and the other a driver, perished with him. Victor Wasdenik and his two brothers, Emil and John, all miners, were also among the victims.

All through the night the rescuing gangs kept at their gruesome task of picking up the dead, who lay strewn along the farther parts of the ill fated tunnel of the Pancoast from off which were the chambers and headings in which they had entered the mine for their days toll. Before midnight twenty-one bodies, including that of Foreman Evans of the Government's rescue car, were placed in an improvised morgue in the engine house near the head of the shaft. At 4 o'clock this morning there had been another garnering of twenty-one additional bodies and then these, one at a time were hoisted to the surface and carried into the morgue. There the company's paymaster, Carl Raymond, claim agent P.A. O'Boyle, George Cooper, secretary of the Miners Local Union, and John E. Jones, outside foreman, were engaged in making identifications and as fast as these were done, the body was passed into one of the score of dead wagons which undertakers from all parts of the valley had lined up. The rapidity with which these were snatched up by the undertakers and their employees, their egresses to get possession of the victims, called forth indignant expressions from the onlookers, some yelling "Body snatchers" at them as their ambulances were hurried a way.

One of the saddest features of, the disaster was the death of Joseph E. Evans, of West Scranton, superintendent of the rescue car attached to the Government rescue station in Wilkes Barre. Evans died a hero of his own heroism after disregarding the warnings of his men. He refused to go to the surface until he collapsed, and he was dead when the carriage reached the mouth.

Charles Enzian, the noted expert in general charge of mine rescue work for the Government, who was at Wilkes Barre rescue station, was also overcome and is in serious condition.

The cause of the disaster was a fire which originated in an unknown manner in the engine house at the foot of the main shaft shortly before noon. For more than one hour employees battled with the flames and it was not until they were beyond control that outside help was summoned.

For some unknown reason the alarm did not reach the men at work in the Dunmore vein, 750 feet below the surface, and they knew nothing of the fire until James Vickers staggered into a chamber and notified the men there. Vickers started back toward the shaft, but he collapsed when he had gone two hundred feet where he was found, lying face downward by the first rescuers who entered the vein.

Vickers was rushed to the surface and heroic work by physicians restored him to consciousness. A group of anxious officials surrounded the dazed man and plied him with questions. "They're all dead," he declared. "They're trapped like rats, the mine is a seething furnace. The supports are burning and the coal is catching fire."

At 5:00 o'clock this morning the rescue party brought to the foot of the shaft twelve more bodies and they too, were sent up the carriage, to be taken away as were the others. All of these victims were found in groups of three, five or six, their faces buried in the dust of the mine roadway or their coats wrapped about their heads,

Here the inside foreman sits at his desk deep within the mine. He was charged with all operations underground. *Courtesy of the author.*

as if that would save them from the insidious poisonous, death dealing after damp, let alone the awful heat that filled the workings, enough of itself to suffocate them.

Dr. Holmes, speaking of the death of Foreman Evans, explained that it was probably due to carbon dioxide poisoning, and stated that in the kind of helmet used by Mr. Evans at the time of his death the exhaled air is regenerated and breathed again. A quantity of oxygen, which is the essential feature of the helmet purifies the air. Mr Roberts said: "A wearer of the helmet under gaseous conditions, who overexerted himself, might meet the fate that befell Mr. Evans. It is like a man running up hill, the supply of fresh air is not sufficient and a man dies from carbon dioxide."

Between 5:00 and 9:00 o'clock this morning, twelve more bodies were hoisted to the surface and four others were being carried out of the tunnel to the foot of the shaft. These bring the total dead, at this hour up to seventy. The indications are that many others are yet to be found, and the grim tragedy of the colliery will be more awful than at first supposed.

Thousands of people were about the mine shaft through the entire morning, many of whom had been there during the entire night. Groups of women seemed to predominate until all the dead found up to noon had been removed, among them many who had lost husbands, fathers, sons and brothers in the awful horror. The immensity of the catastrophe seemed to pacify these, until they were led away to their homes, nearby, then their shrieks and cries were heard, adding further poignancy to the grief of those who watched them go. Many out of the same home perished. Victor, John and Emil Wadzenick, brothers, and Leon Poseva, a cousin, living together in the home of John Schenko, brother-in-law of the Wadzenik's, are among the dead, and when these four bodies were placed side by side in the miners humble home there was the most painful grief. In other homes occurred the same sad scene. The grief-stricken mother of Steve Obrosky arrived at the mine morgue in time to see her son's body loaded into a dead wagon. The frenzied woman ran after the wagon, demanding, with heart breaking shrieks, the return of her dead, but the undertaker, heedless of her cries, drove away.

Squads of state troopers were early on the ground today, to assist the local and Scranton police detail in holding the crowds in check. Coroner Saltry, accompanied by an officer of the district attorneys office, spent the whole morning at the mine and will join a thorough investigation that is to determine the responsibility for the terrible calamity.

On May 8, 1911, the coroner's jury, headed by Edward F. Blewitt (foreman), Enoch Williams, Robert Gillard, John P. McDonough, William E. Lewis and James Grady, brought forth this verdict:

That John Baravalla, Louis Korman, Lawerence Reitz, et al. came to their death on the morning of April 7, 1911, through inhalation of carbon monoxide, the direct cause of which was the burning of a hoisting engine house at the head of the North Slope in the No. 2 Dunmore vein of the Pancoast colliery, the flames from which communicated with contiguous timbers in the entrance to the engine house and communicated from there to the roof supports and cars in the main haulage way, causing vast volumes of smoke to be driven into the China vein by the great velocity of the air current from the fan. We declare that the cause of the fire is unknown and have no hesitation in saying that we believe overzealousness of the management to put out the fire in the engine house, and forgetfulness to a degree for the safety of the men in the mine contributed largely to making this accident so appalling.

2.
EXPLOSION IN THE MINES

WADESVILLE COLLIERY
"A FEARFUL EXPLOSION"
WADESVILLE, PENNSYLVANIA
MAY 9, 1877

One of the most dangerous accidents that can happen in the process of mining coal is the explosion of fire damp, better known as light carbureted hydrogen. It is lighter than air and is given off by the opening of a seam of coal. It is found in the roof of the breast or chamber. You can't see it, feel it or smell it; its most dangerous aspect is that it is highly explosive.

On Wednesday, May 9, 1877, at the Wadesville Colliery about three miles north of Pottsville an explosion of fire damp took the lives of six miners in a devastating explosion. The Wadesville Shaft Colliery has been in operation since 1868. The shaft, which is 664 feet deep, reaches down into the mammoth vein at this point. The shaft is used as the coal outlet and also for air intake. There is a second shaft that is used as an air uptake and as an egress in case of an emergency.

The May 9, 1877 *Pottsville Evening Chronicle* reported this event from the scene of the accident by sending their reporter and a telegraph operator to the shaft. Following is the report that was sent to the newspaper office.

> This morning about half past 9 o'clock a fearful explosion of fire damp occurred at Wadesville Shaft, near Pottsville. How it happened is not yet known, but is supposed there was a large fall of coal, which forced a lot of gas out of a breast that had been

Wadesville Colliery, "A Fearful Explosion"

An interesting view of the Wadesville Colliery and how it looked during the accident on May 9, 1877. Wadesville, Pennsylvania. *Courtesy of the author.*

The Wadesville Colliery showing the slope and shaft head frames, the pump house and engine house. *Courtesy of the Historical Society of Schuylkill County.*

idle some time past, and this becoming ignited from the lamps of the men, caused the explosion. John Durkin, residing in Saint Clair, was instantly killed by one of the flying timbers which were hurled around by the shock. He leaves a wife and one child. William Kirk, living in the same place, was also killed. He leaves a wife and three children. Thomas Connors, Joseph Milward, Herbert Moore and Benjamin Mosely were penned in by a strong barricade of the fallen coal. All the available miners were immediately sent to rescue them, if possible, but the air was so impregnated it was impossible for them to work more than a minute or two at a time. All of them now have been taken out dead. They must have been literally roasted, as their bodies, upon the arrival at the top of the

DEATH IN THE MINES

Every day the fire boss checked every working place for fire damp (methane gas). Here he places his safety lamp to the roof to check for the gas. *Courtesy of the author.*

One of the dangers in a working mine was the fall of coal. Here a group of miners survey the damage. *Courtesy of the author.*

shaft, presented a sickening sight, with their clothing burned from their bodies, their hair from their heads and the flesh hanging in shreds from their bodies. Connors is a newly married man, Milward was unmarried, Mosely was married but leaves no children, and Moore leaves a wife and seven small children. Besides these who were killed were a number of badly burned, Viz.: John Reese, John Gleavey, Patrick Gibbons, Dennis Brennan, John McAtee and Abraham Jones. Most of them are young unmarried men.

The scene in front of the shaft beggars description. As the cage comes up to the scene of the shaft the women rush forward to see if any of their husbands, brothers or sons are among the number killed or injured. The mouth of the shaft is crowded with a throng of men, women and children, and when one of their relations come up from the mine injured, or perhaps killed, it is indeed heartrending to witness their tears and hear the cries of distress.

Wadesville Colliery, "A Fearful Explosion"

The news of the explosion spread like wild fire and as all the people living in the vicinity have relations working there, they immediately rushed pell mell to the mouth of the shaft. For a long time it was impossible to learn anything definite and the anxiety of the watchers cannot be described. When any one came out of the shaft they anxiously gathered around to learn, if possible, some particulars. Each breath of air brought with it some rumor which was distorted to suit the fancy of the excited brains of the persons gathered around. The wildest imaginable rumors prevailed, and many persons predicted a second Avondale disaster, but happily although the loss of life was terrible it did not equal that of Avondale.

About ten o'clock yesterday morning, rumors of a terrible disaster at Wadesville Shaft, began to float through St. Clair, but for a time nothing definite could be learned. At last, however, these rumors began to assume a tangible shape, and it became generally known that a fearful explosion had taken place at the shaft. As the major portion of the residents of the town have friends employed at this colliery, the excitement that ensued may be [better] imagined than described when the news was whispered around. Never in its history has St. Clair witnessed such a day. Men left their shops and stores, women ceased their household duties and the children left the school room, all proceeding in a terrible state of excitement and suspense to the shaft, to learn if any of their loved ones had been injured. All the population of the town concentrated at that point, and as the rumors were more or less distorted by the time they reached the ears of the interested parties, in their excited imaginations they saw the whole colliery in ruins, and the men slaughtered by the wholesale. Some of the uninjured miners had by this time arrived at the top of the shaft, and around these anxiously clustered the mothers, and daughters and wives, each all desiring to know what fates those they held most dear had met with. And here the first reliable information was gleaned. It was learned that a serious accident had indeed taken place, and that many men were injured and killed.

The exact cause of the accident will probably never be known. The supposition is that a fall occurred in an old breast near by, and a large quantity of standing gas, was consequently forced into the other breasts, and becoming ignited by the lighted lamps of the miners, caused the explosion. This is the theory of the mine inspector and others who visited the scene. The explosion was a terrible one, but the amount of damage done on the inside of the colliery was not as large as might have been expected. Large pieces of timbers of the thickness of a horses body were in many cases blown the distance of fifty yards.

John Durkin, of St. Clair, who was in the vicinity of the explosion, was instantly killed by being struck by a small portable fan, which was blown from a considerable distance. His body was the first to be recovered and was found to be terribly disfigured. He had a large and deep gash on the temple, his lip slit and a deep wound in his throat, and is supposed his neck broken. His leg and arm were also fractured. He leaves a wife and one child. Durkin was much respected, and leaves a large circle of friends to mourn his untimely end. He was a gallant soldier during the war.

William Kirk, residing in the same place, was badly disfigured and must have been blown about terribly, as his boots were torn from his feet. A large lump of coal weighing a couple of hundred pounds fell on his chest, and from under his "butty" Edward Farrell labored bravely, in the midst of the commotion, to rescue him, but in vain as he died before it could be removed. Kirk leaves a wife and three children. He was a very respectable young man and a prominent member of the St. Clair Light Infantry.

Herbert Moore, Joseph Milward, Thomas Conners and Benjamin Moasely who were the nearest to the scene of the explosion, were blown around like so many straws in a whirlwind and the shock bringing down a fall of coal, erected a strong barrier between them and the outer world. As usual in such cases, after the explosion, the air became so impure that a human being could not possibly exist in it for the space of two minutes, and had they not been otherwise injured they were obliged to succumb to this fell destroyer. A number of willing hands immediately set to work to rescue the bodies, but with no hope of finding the men alive, as they themselves were forced to desist every few minutes, and when they fell to the ground were carried to the pure air in the rear, and their places supplied by fresh men. Thus the work continued.

The body of Herbert Moore was the first recovered. It was literally baked and presented a most horrible appearance. He was dead long before he had been reached. Moore leaves a wife and seven small children to mourn his tragic death. He was for many years one of the best respected residents of St. Clair, and his loss will be felt by the community.

The body of Joseph Milward was next discovered. His appearance would indicate that he was suffocated by the impure air, as his body bore no evidence of being disfigured. Milward was unmarried. He was [a] quiet, unassuming youth, and never earned the ill will of anybody.

To the eye of the *Chronicle* reporter, who witnessed the removal of the body of Thomas Connors from the debris in the shaft, was presented a most sickening sight. The boots were blown off his feet, which now hung suspended from his legs by thin, thread like pieces of flesh. The whole top of his head was laid open, and the brains scattered in every direction. A receptacle had to be provided in which they were conveyed to his home. Even those accustomed to such sights drew back in horror at the frightful appearance of the body. Connors had been married but a few months, and the blow is a terrible one to his young wife. He was generally beloved on account of his inoffensive and pleasant disposition, and his loss is sincerely mourned by all who knew him.

The body of Benjamin Moasely was not found until half past twelve o'clock last night. He was found at some distance from the scene of the explosion, and must have been blown about considerably, as one of his boots were found six or seven hours before his body. His person was not at all disfigured, so it is probable that he met his death from suffocation. Moasley was married but leaves no children. He resided in Wadesville and always bore a good character.

Besides those killed were a number badly burned, James Leddy, a married man of St. Clair, is so horribly burned that his recovery is extremely doubtful. John Gleavy, single, St. Clair, is terribly burned, and has the whole of his scalp is removed. Abraham Jones is also badly burned about the face and body. John Reese, Patrick Gibbons, James McAtee and Dennis Brennan are more or less burned.

About 10 o'clock this morning Deputy Coroner William G. Burwell, with a Coroner's jury, proceeded to the different residences to examine the bodies of the deceased. Coroner Quail will take their verdict in Wadesville at 1 o'clock today.

The story of Edward Weaklam, who had a miraculous escape from death, gives additional particulars of the great disaster. He stated that he was a butty of Herbert Moore, one of the victims, and was on a low platform, shoveling coal into a mine car, when there came a rush of burning gas down the air course like a flash of lightning. He dropped from the platform and fell full length on the gangway track, grasped

DEATH IN THE MINES

A view of the gangway leading into the largest vein of coal in the world, the Mammoth Vein. Shenandoah, Pennsylvania. *Courtesy of the Historical Society of Schuylkill County.*

an iron rail and held on, and the explosion hurled the car from the track and threw it against the wall and shielded him from the flame. He escaped, but on either side of him men were roasted alive while at work. Weaklam lay still for a moment and then jumped up and crawled along the passage to escape the deadly after damp. His lamp was out, and [he] groped his way through the debris in the dark until he heard voices of other miners and he soon reached a place of safety.

On May 11, the report continued with the testimony of the witnesses during the coroner's inquest.

Yesterday afternoon about two o'clock Coroner Quail arrived at St. Clair for the purpose of holding an inquest on the bodies of the men who had been killed by the Wadesville Shaft Explosion. The men picked to act as the jury were Moses Parkins, foreman, John Siney, R.C. Boyer, George Rodgers, William Yeo and Joseph Townsend, and they proceeded to view the bodies. The first witness called was William Hurtman, of St. Clair, who was Durkin's butty at the time of the accident. He told a very disconnected story, but from what we glean the following: They had been working an airway which run parallel with Lundy's gangway, getting out so much of the lose coal as possible. For the few weeks preceding the explosion they had from two to four feet of gas in their place, out on the day of the explosion they had none whatever. Mr. Herbert, the boss had obliged them to use safety lamps, and these were discarded but a few days prior to the accident. Witness

56

was eating his dinner between ten and eleven o'clock, when the explosion occurred. Durkin was at this time some distance away in the gangway getting some logs. He had hardly left the witness presence two minutes when the explosion took place. He never saw the inspector at the colliery in his life. When the wind had passed he picked himself up and found the dead body of Durkin lying in the gangway.

Edward Herbert, late inside boss of Wadesville Colliery, was next examined. He and the new boss Watkins, were out on their rounds through the colliery, and when about two hundred yards from the scene of the explosion they heard a heavy fall of coal or rock. In about two seconds after the fall the gas fired. They misjudged the direction from whence the sound of the fall came, and went eastward, but quickly found out their mistake and proceeded westward. They first found the body of John Durkin lying in the gangway. A short distance farther on they met the after damp, and soon came upon Edward Farrell, who said his butty, Kirk, was lying under a lump of coal in the breast. The fire boss and a number of other men had come up by this time and he sent them in trying to rescue Kirk. The witness then proceeded up another gangway and hollered but received no answer. Finding himself sinking from the effects of bad air he retraced his steps. I found it impossible to live in such air and the men who were rescuing Kirk were obliged to desist. Boards of canvas were erected into batteries so as to carry the current of the air, and by this means dissolve the force of the after damp. In this manner they reached Kirk and found him dead with a lump of coal 18 inches thick lying broken on his body. After awhile we reached Milward, when they were obliged to desist from their labors and wait the coming of fresh men. The body of Benjamin Mosely was found this morning. The particular place where the fall occurred was not examined, but from his knowledge of the locality the witness said it must have been in one of the old worked out places. Witness thought that Mr. Parton became inspector of mines in 1875. He had visited the colliery six or seven times since then. The inspector generally went through the mine after an accident and suggested improvements. If gas was found in any of the old workings he gave me instructions to have it removed. A man could not have lived ten minutes in that place, and even if everything were handy, it would not reach them with the air inside of half an hour. When the miners heard the fall, if they had the presence of mind enough to quench their lights, the explosion would not have occurred. I have given instructions to the men to always do this. If the men had used their safety lamps as they were ordered, the explosion would not have occurred. The mine inspector ordered me to have the airway widened, and when it was finished he came and examined it.

In a special dispatch to the *Pottsville Evening Chronicle*, some of the jury complained that some of the witnesses were afraid to testify for fear of being discharged. This was brought about by an article that was published in the *Miners Journal*.

After a lengthy investigation the inspector of the mines Mr. Parton stated the probable cause of this catastrophe was caused by a large section of coal falling from the loose seven foot vein, which in turn opened up a large pocket of gas. The men involved were in the process of robbing the coal back from this area. In this process the men were told not to leave the ventilating door in the gangway open. This door was considered very important to the ventilation of this part of the gangway, and special instructions were given to the miners and drivers that this door was not to be left open longer than absolutely needed for the passage of men or wagons. No coal was to be taken from within a certain distance of the door. The door had been further secured by timbers near it a few days before. On the 8th of May the door was removed by the men then at work. At sometime on the 9th the fall of coal occurred and the gas was sent flowing down through the gangway and into the area where Herbert Moore was pushing an empty car, when his naked light ignited the gas causing the explosion.

What amount of gas had accumulated in the portion of the intake and return air courses deprived of ventilation is of course unknown, but if it had been entirely filled with fire damp, in an explosive condition, unquestionably all the men then at work in that section would have been lost.

Six lives were lost through a want of foresight and intelligence in utilizing the means that were amply furnished for their security. Mining is necessarily a dangerous calling, but necessary dangers are very much increased by a lack of intelligent cooperation on the part of the workmen. In the earnest hope that miners who may read the report may realize the importance of the fact that it is far better to obey orders of their superiors than to trust their own judgment.

THE EAST BROOKSIDE COLLIERY, "EXPLOSION!"
TOWER CITY, PENNSYLVANIA
AUGUST 2, 1913

It was 11:20 a.m. on August 2, 1913, the day Charles Portland, a mining contractor, was hired by the Pennsylvania Reading Railroad and Coal and Iron Company to drive a one-thousand-foot tunnel from the number four to the number five vein in the East Brookside mine. He employed nine men and a few laborers to do the work on this Saturday morning. They were cleaning up most of the debris that was left over from the blasting that took place on Friday, August 1. On the surface, the sound of a muffled explosion was heard and immediately everyone knew that something had gone wrong. Anyone working nearby who turned to look toward the slope saw smoke billowing from the open ventilator fan and out of the mouth of the slope. Men ran to the entrance and immediately formed a rescue party and descended into the depths of the mine.

Twenty minutes later another muffled explosion was heard. Twenty men lost their lives in this tragic accident and from this day on Saturday, August 2, 1913, was known as Black Saturday, Schuylkill County's worst mining disaster. The following story is filled with the horrors, dangers and heroic efforts that the men who worked at East Brookside experienced during this tragedy.

The first reports of the accident reached the public by the evening issue of the *Pottsville Daily Republican* on August 2, and intense reports would follow this terrible catastrophe from beginning to end.

DEATH IN THE MINES

Miners sitting on a flat car waiting to enter the concrete reinforced slope at the Brookside Colliery, Tower City, Pennsylvania. *Courtesy of the Historical Society of Schuylkill County.*

The headline stated "Seven Dead and 50 Entombed at East Brookside."

Eight men have been removed from the East Brookside mine at 3:15 o'clock this afternoon and the number seven were dead. The known dead are Howard and Harry Hand, Thomas Behney, of Reinerton, Daniel McGinley, fire Boss of Tower City, one foreigner who's [sic] head was blown off and the other two not identified. Fire boss Schoffstall the only one rescued alive is authority for the statement that there were at least 30 in number 5 working where the explosion occurred. And it is believed all have perished. Superintendent John Lawerence and head boss Farrell are among the men in the mine and are believed to have been killed.

The explosion was caused by men blowing into a pocket of gas and the gas igniting from one of the lamps of the men. The first explosion was followed quickly by a second of greater force. Immediately other workmen were hurried to the stricken mine and recovered the bodies of the two Hand boys and reported that five others were lying with them. Behney and McGinley were brought out next and then followed two unidentified men and a third who had his head blown off.

The explosion occurred shortly after 12 o'clock and word was sent to officials of the company in Pottsville who responded immediately but gave no inkling to the public of the horrible catastrophe which was evident at first reports. Later no information could be obtained at the local headquarters as they claim that they received no word since the officials were called to the ill-fated colliery. Gen. Mgr. Richards, Div. Supt. Kearcher and other officials are on the scene.

After the first explosion fire boss Daniel McGinley, Chief boss John Farrell and Supt. John Lawrence went into the workings and it was then that the second explosion occurred. As McGinley's remains were recovered it is believed that the others who were with him met similar fates.

Miners and others who visited the mines are certain that the death list will reach at least a score. The colliery was not working today, but a large force of repairmen were at work. Had the explosion occurred on another day, the list of the dead would have been considerably greater.

General Manager Richards arrived on the scene shortly after it happened, he being summoned from Pottsville, together with a number of officials. An inkling of the terrible nature of the catastrophe was given out when all of the oldest and most experienced miners from Lincoln, Good Spring, and even as far south as Branchdale were summoned.

East Brookside colliery is one of the best operations of the P. & R.C.&I. co. [Pennsylvania and Reading Coal and Iron Company] located on the mountain north of Tower City, in the west end of the county. The coal from this colliery is of such good quality that it sells from fifty cents to a dollar more per ton than the product from other collieries. It has been one of the best managed and equipped with the most modern appliances. The company had been pushing arrangements for some months for the erection of an additional breaker to take care of largely increased output resulting from new openings principally on the north side of the mountain in the Hegins Valley. The colliery employs about 800 men and boys ordinarily and can ship 100,000 tons a month.

The second force of rescuers who went down into the mine reported that there were no signs of life. As the colliery was not working today it is not known how many were in the ill fated working but it is conservatively estimated that there are not less than a dozen, mostly repair men while the number may go as high as fifty.

All the doctors in that section were hurried to the mine and it was impossible to secure a physician anywhere outside of the colliery. The Reading company immediately rushed all available mine ambulances and rescue corps and apparatus to the mine and the rescue car was ordered to report for service at the mine. The towns in the vicinity of the operation were almost completely deserted.

On Monday, August 4, 1913, the *Pottsville Daily Republican* headlines once again reported the tragedy unfolding at East Brookside.

19 DEAD, 1 DYING, LEAVING 51 ORPHANS AS A RESULT OF E. BROOKSIDE.

The magnificent heights of the Broad Mountain at one of the grandest and most picturesque points in Schuylkill County today look down upon the worst tragedy in the history of the county. Looking down from the mountain top at the East Brookside colliery, the scene of the frightful explosion of Saturday, are here and there houses marked with black crape, telling eloquently and pitilessly the story of nineteen sons of the Williams Valley who gave up their lives, some of them in the cause of the great industrial work this region must perform as its share of the burdens of this world, and others, who with all the heroism which has caused man's name to be handed down to history, gave up their lives in a vain effort to save fellow workmen who were practically unknown to these martyrs of duty. In the pages of the Williams Valley history these names will go down as the heroes of the twentieth century. Daniel McGinley, Henry Murphy, Harry Schoffstall, Howard Hand, Thomas Behney and Jacob Kopenhaver.

In fatalities where large numbers meet death it is usual to see a long list of seriously and slightly injured, but with the East Brookside catastrophe there is no such list to set forth. There is just one name on the list, that of Harry Schoffstall, all others are "The Dead."

The first explosion came at 11:20 o'clock. That is the time which the disordered watches of the dead tunnel men give as insurmountable and convincing evidence. The second explosion came about 20 minutes later. That is guess work. There is no stopping of watches when the second killing blast came because that carried with it chiefly the scorching flames and deadly poisonous after damp. Outside of the tunnel men who were caught in the first explosion the deaths were chiefly due to after damp poisoning which was strange to say was less pitiless with the mules in the ill fated working, most of which were found living when the second body of rescuers penetrated the dangerous ruins which the explosion had left.

There were other heroes besides those who went to their deaths. It is estimated that there were about a hundred of them. They formed

The East Brookside Colliery, "Explosion!"

In this photo a rescue crew helps another miner who has been overcome by gas. The men wear the Draeger oxygen rescue helmet widely used in the mines. *Courtesy of the author.*

the second bunch of rescuers, but were better equipped for the work in hand and had less dangers to encounter, although that fact was not known to them when they were swiftly lowered down the steeped pitched slope and saw the daylight fade away as the rope was reeled out and let them down into the chamber of death. They took their lives in their hands in an effort to bring back the ill-fated victims of the two frightful explosions, but fortunately the demands of the Grim Reaper had been appeased and they returned again to their comrades and their families, with blanched faces showing behind the coating of black coal dirt and told in husky voices of the sights they had seen within.

They saw nothing but death and ruin. They saw their closest companions and warmest friends and comrades stretched out in death amid the ruins which had followed the devastating work of the dynamite and gas explosions in No. 5 level. They were accustomed to sights such as the East Brookside exposed to their view on Saturday.

But their feelings were concealed when there was work to be done. With Draeger Oxygen Helmets on their heads to protect them from the afterdamp, they penetrated the workings unmindful of the dangers which constantly confronted them. They pierced the heading studded with overhanging rocks and blocked by torn timbers and debris. Any minute they were threatened with a death just as horrible as that which was meted out to their comrades, but they hesitated not an instant. These lions of the coal mine pushed their way through the heading to the tunnel and traveled a mile or more underground to make sure that no living creature remained whom it might be possible to rescue. Then they brought their story to the surface.

Those at the mouth of the tender slope which the rescuers had descended, awaiting with hearts half stopped, hopping for the best, but

DEATH IN THE MINES

INJURED BEING TREATED IN MINE HOSPITAL.

Left: In this photograph a miner receives first aid in an underground first-aid station. *Courtesy of the author.*

Below: An interesting entrance to a mine slope. *Courtesy of the Historical Society of Schuylkill County.*

the story that the rescuers had to tell was only that the worst had happened. There was not one word of cheer, not one tone of hope as the first of this rescuing force came back to the surface. In anguish they informed the waiting miners at the mouth of the slope. "All are dead."

It couldn't be these experienced miners knew that it was a fearful explosion and a fearful tragedy but they could not believe that all had perished. Such a thing was impossible. East Brookside was one of the best equipped mines in the region, one of the safest; it was impossible that a score of men could be wiped out in one scourging breath. They almost laughed at the fears of the rescuers, but their hearts nevertheless beat slower, their faces became whiter and more drawn. They had hoped for the best, they were told the worst, and now they feared the worst.

They had not long to wait to be convinced that the worst was only too true for soon two bodies were brought out. They were two of the rescuing force. Then came two more, one of them Schoffstall. He breathed.

"He lives," they whispered in hushed tones. "He lives, they are not all dead," went up the hopeful but hushed cry, but it was the only ray of hope which came to the eyes or ears of the stricken Williams Valley populace on that ill-fated day except when the unconscious form of Supt. John Lorenz was brought up the cage in the slope entrance of the mine.

He lived also. Then there might be hopes for some of the others. Best of all, the superintendent, known and beloved by every man, woman and child in the valley, did not seem to be mortally hurt. But already most of the rest had been brought to the surface, and there were no hopes for many to be saved.

Foreman Farrell was with the Supt. Lorenz and it was hoped that he, too had escaped the fury of the explosion, but these hopes were quickly dashed when the dead body of the popular colliery boss was brought to the surface.

In pairs they were brought out of the ill-fated mine until the number sixteen had been recovered. There were still two more bodies inside Fessler and Farley, but even the absence of the actual proof of their deaths gave no consolation because it was appreciated by these trained miners that they had no chance to get out alive. Some would have welcomed the sight of their remains so certain were they that the toll of death had claimed them.

The news of the catastrophe quickly spread to the towns nestling in this beautiful part of the imposing Williams Valley. They came from all over. From Tremont some hurried. Every woman and child was ready and anxious to perform some service but they found none to perform beyond comforting the families of the dead men. A half dozen physicians were at the mouth of the working and even they were helpless in view of the fearful effects of the catastrophe. They could not help the dead, they were there to administer to the living and the injured but there were no living and injured to be treated. Every body brought up was that of an unfortunate worker who was beyond all earthly assistance.

Orderly and with training which will not be found anywhere outside of the coal region did this body of men, women and children wait for the news from within. Among the waiting throng were the families and relatives of the ill-fated workmen.

Identification of the American dead of the workmen was made in the mines before they were brought to the surface and when the bodies were brought the word was quietly passed of the identity of the victims and with hysterical sobs mothers and wives, sons and daughters, brothers and sisters were led away in the arms of sympathizing friends. They had heard the worst. The fearful proportion of the disaster faded from their minds, they remembered only that the hand of death had fallen upon their own household, that hope had been extinguished, that life was made less worth living.

The sunshine had gone out of their lives, the past seemed a pleasant dream, the future loomed up dark and uninviting. In that sorrowing stream of bended heads who heard the names of their own called out there was probably not one who would have gladly given up their own lives to bring back those of the hero dead.

The ambulances which had gathered to perform a work of mercy for the injured were converted into dead wagons for the undertakers and it seemed that there was a never ending string of these black and heart sickening vehicles passing up and down the steep and rough mountain road from the valley of peace and beauty to the mountain of gloom and horror.

Those who waited down in the valley stifled back their sobs and merely shook their heads, one to the other, and sadly echoed "Another one." The catastrophe which had befallen them was too great for them to properly appreciate the horror of it, to fully comprehend what it all meant; they simply knew that their own little towns were the scene of one of the most heart rending accidents that has ever occurred in the anthracite region.

All evening crowds gathered along the streets and there was only one topic of conversation. Here and there one of the rescuing force was compelled to tell the story over and over again. They told the story without exaggeration, without any effort for thrill, their recital seemed more like the sermon of some pastor than the thrilling account one might expect from lion hearted men who had faced death and who had seen death and know they may someday have a similar fate visited upon them.

The fate of Fessler and Farley was perhaps the chief topic. There was some hope for them, although the only real hope seemed to be that their dead bodies had not been recovered. Experienced miners who worked at E. Brookside were encouraged to tell listeners how it might be possible for the two men to have escaped. These men seemed anxious to give some hope and they endeavored to solve the problem of how it might be possible that these two might be living and just as there appeared to be some gleam of hope some experienced miner would sadly shake his head.

There was a story in circulation that the two unaccounted for bosses had made their way through an old working and had come out in the vicinity of Rausch Gap. It gave some hope but this hope was dispelled when some miners pointed out that it would not have been necessary for them to have taken such a route and, as Farley and Fessler were as well acquainted with the mine as any other living man, they would have known the best and the quickest way to get out.

Again the story had been circulated that tapping had been heard from behind a wall of rock. This hope was quickly shattered when it was pointed out that most of the deaths had been caused by black damp and that the men could not be alive in that section where the rapping was reported to have been heard.

Again in an effort to convince themselves that there might be some hope miners brought the news to the surface that Fessler had written a message that he intended to go down into an air hole to make an inspection. This is customary in the mine. "Might he not have gone down and escaped with his life?" "No" the heartless truth would say if he had been down there he certainly would have been killed the same as the others.

Then there arose the hope that perhaps the dead might only be sixteen as the remains of the missing men might be among the five unidentified and who were supposed to be foreign workmen. Friends of the missing men were sent to the colliery office to endeavor to make an identification. It was proved that the body of Fessler at least, was not among the dead recovered because on one hand Fessler had two thumbs and there was no such a hand among the dead awaiting identification. It was also convincing to the friends of Farley that he was not among those unidentified.

THE STORY OF THE EXPLOSION

Thursday afternoon when quitting time came the 500 or more employees at the East Brookside took their cans and made their way

DEATH IN THE MINES

Miners drilling into rock face to fire a shot while driving a new gangway. *Courtesy of the Historical Society of Schuylkill County.*

down the steep mountainside to remain at home until Monday as the colliery, along with the other P. & R.C.&I. operations had been ordered to suspend for the week with four days worked. While the miners and laborers were not on duty, still there were some who reported for work to make some necessary inspection, do a little repair work and, most unfortunate of all, complete the tunnel, the tunnel which was being driven to open a new source of supply of coal.

The tunnel was being driven by Contractor Charles Portland, of Pottsville. It was about finished. Saturday's work was expected to about finish it with the exception of a little straightening out minor details which were to be looked after before it could be turned over.

Friday night a gang of expert rockmen were at work and had fired a number of shots and brought down a large quantity of rock. To clear away this debris the mucker foreman and his gang consisting of nine men in all reported for work Saturday morning.

It is said that they took 175 pounds of dynamite in the tunnel with them. It is this dynamite that is believed to have been the cause of the death of nineteen men.

These men were not supposed to fire off any shots and for this reason there is a division of opinion as to what really caused the first explosion. It is all speculation in this direction. One theory is that a blasting cap which had been dropped in the debris the night before and was unexploded was struck by the shovel of one of the gang of muckers and that it exploded and perhaps set off the 175 pounds of dynamite.

It was this explosion which is believed to have caused the death of the nine workmen in the tunnel gang, the mucker boss, the blacksmith and his helper and six laborers. It is this explosion also which is thought to have liberated a large pocket of gas and caused it to penetrate the connecting headings until it exploded just as the first crowd of rescuers reached the bottom of No. 5 level and were coming from the slope to investigate the tunnel explosion.

Just what caused this second explosion is not known, although it is the general impression that the fire from the dynamite explosion which probably smoldered for some time was the cause of the ignition of a large body of gas.

There was a story to the effect that the rescuing force went into the mine with carbide lights which are not provided with safety devices. This is denied as it is claimed by Schoffstall that they were all equipped with safety lamps. Schoffstall says he was making his way along the heading towards the tunnel with McGinley and Murphy, when suddenly he was swept from his feet, there was a flash and a frightful roar and he and his two companions were hurled to the ground. He managed to struggle to his feet and escaped the poisonous fumes of the after damp but he was really more dead than alive when recovered and it is not thought that he would long survive.

As the rescuing force was made up of some of the best miners in the anthracite fields it is not thought that the explosion of gas was due to any neglect of their own. Most of them were officials whose business it was to meet and solve and avert such accidents and it is not likely that they would have thrust their lives into certain death which they must have known would be a penalty of any carelessness.

On the other hand there is a theory that a sudden volume of gas swept down upon this little rescuing party as they were making their way up along the heading and that did not give them the opportunity to escape before their safety lamps ignited it.

While the safety lamp is intended for use in gaseous mines, it is not entirely proof against gas. The presence of gas is quickly detected by the lamp and when its presence is found in great volume it is necessary for the miner to retire before the gauze becomes heated or else there is a danger of causing an explosion. There is a belief among some of the miners that a great current of gas suddenly swept upon the rescuing band and there was no time given them to make their escape.

DEATH IN THE MINES

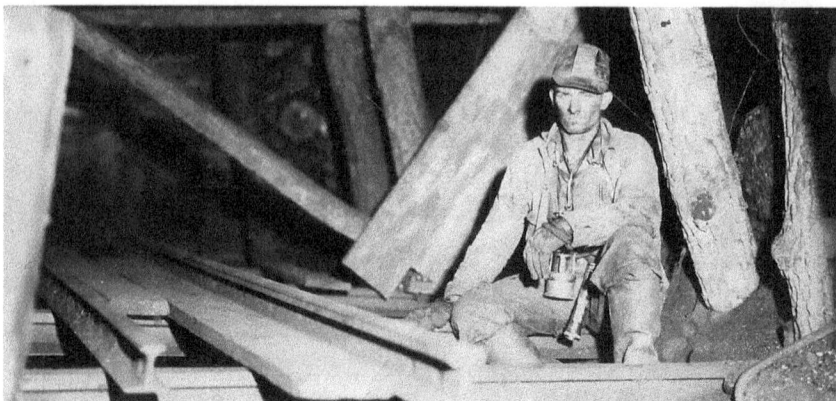

An excellent view of a miner sitting in a heading with his safety lamp. *Courtesy of the author.*

The top man signals the engine house to lower the car down the slope. *Courtesy of the Historical Society of Schuylkill County.*

An interesting view of the entrance into a slope. Note the sharp degree of pitch. *Courtesy of the Historical Society of Schuylkill County.*

The East Brookside Colliery, "Explosion!"

The first explosion [was] made known to those on the surface by a deadened report and a puff of dust from the fan house and from the mouth of the slope. The experienced mining men on hand knew at once what it meant and with haste they entered the slope. Frank Unger was among the band but just as he was about to step into the car to be lowered with the six other men he was directed to go to the lamp house and assist in getting lamps ready for the force of workers to follow the first relief. He obeyed directions and to his discipline he owes his life.

It seemed to those on the surface that the rescuers had been in the mine about twenty minutes when there was another muffled report heard and another puff of dust came from the slope and the fan house.

It was appreciated that an accident of unusual proportions had occurred and immediately a second rescuing party was made up. They knew the fate that had probably met the force that went into the mine but this did not deter one single man and they entered the mine car at the mouth of the slope. The signal was given to the engineer, the engine started out with a puff and a rumble, the big drum began unwinding its great length of 2500 feet of steel rope and the car disappeared into the black cavern, the lights carried by the rescuer remaining in view but a moment when they disappeared from view down the steep incline which pitches 80 degrees. Down they went 1200 feet to the fifth level, within one level to the bottom of the mine. The drum ceased to revolve, the engine was silent, until after what seemed like an age, there was a signal to hoist. Up came some of the rescuing force. To the anxious ones waiting at the mouth of the slope they reported that a fearful calamity had occurred. That they had recovered several dead and had seen at least five more lying in one heap.

The two Draeger helmets at the East Brookside were pressed into service and two miners experienced in their use harnessed up, the tank of oxygen strapped to their shoulders with tubes connecting it with the head piece. They looked like some hideous being thus equipped. Down they were rushed with the rescuers, just a few minutes after the second explosion occurred and soon they were penetrating gas filled sections which could not have been entered without the use of this device. Word was telephoned to other near by collieries and the Draeger outfits from these collieries were hurried to the ill-fated mine and more heroes were harnessed up and sent down to explore the workings.

DEATH IN THE MINES

Most of the men were found in the tunnel or in the immediate vicinity of it, the second rescuing force being found but a short distance away from the slope. The rescuers hunted in vain for Supt. Lorenz and Foreman Farrell for hours before they were finally located in a heading farther from the slope than the tunnel.

They were in the mine before the first explosion occurred making an inspection of the work which had been done. It is always the practice of the fire bosses and foreman [to] report for work when the collieries aren't working and to go through the inside workings thoroughly to see that they are in the proper condition, as they can do more effective work when the mines are not in operation.

Lorenz was one of the best known and most efficient of the mining experts of the Reading Company and who had held the position of superintendent of the West End Collieries for about twenty years was in a small heading with Farrell. When the first explosion occurred there was no way of knowing where they were and for this reason it was a difficult matter to locate them.

Supt. Kaercher and several other rescuers in their search walked about a mile in a circuitous route before they came across the pair. Lorenz was first discovered. He was conscious and was crawling through the debris in the dark along the side of the heading.

"Don't bother with me, Lorenz." Mr. Kaercher recognized him and asked him if he was badly hurt.

"I am sore and used up but never mind me, go hunt Jack he needs help more than I do." He referred to Farrell who had been stricken dead at his side. They pushed on to the point directed by Lorenz and there found Farrell, but he was not in need of their help, he was dead.

They hurried back to Lorenz and picked him up and carried him toward the shaft to which there was an easier and quicker exit than by way of the slope. They brought him up to the surface in safety. There were prayers of thanksgiving that he had been saved, but there were no cheers, no shouts, of exultation. It was no time for cheers even if one man had been saved, even if he was one of the most beloved men in this region. He was placed aboard the Black Diamond after receiving temporary treatment by the doctors who had responded to the call for help. He was hurried to Pottsville, not thought by those at the colliery to be mortally injured but when he arrived at the hospital it was quickly apparent that he received his death blow in the mine over which he had supervision for so many years and he slowly sank during Saturday night until death came at an early hour Sunday morning with his family by his bedside.

John Endise, a blacksmith employed by contractor Portland was the only member of the tunnel gang found alive by the helmeted rescuers. He was brought to the surface and put on the train for Pottsville but he died before the train reached Keffers and the remains were taken off and sent back to Reiner City.

With every appearance of the car at the mouth of the slope as it emerged from the black depths there was a crowding forward to see the dead removed there from until finally the count had reached sixteen. Then the crowd began to disperse. The relatives of Messrs. Farley and Fessler were prevailed upon to their homes and when twilight came the only ones around the slope were the officials of the company, the miners, a few employees who had not been on duty and the "Republican" reporters.

Every section of the affected workings had been explored thoroughly and no trace of the two missing men could be obtained. Near the ill fated tunnel a wall of rock about 50 feet in length had been brought down by the force of the explosion and the rescuers reached the conclusion that Farley and Fessler were buried underneath that or behind it. A force was put to work at once to clear away this fall and this work was prosecuted with a vim and with just as much fervor as though the rescuers hoped to find their two comrades alive under the fall.

As all of the dead had been either found in the tunnel or near the mouth of it, it was not supposed that Fessler and Farley could be far away from that point and therefore the conclusion was reached that they were buried under this fallen rock, although as they had been in the mine before the first explosion occurred, it was recognized as possible that they might have been at some far removed point. Farrell and Lorenz were about 50 feet away from the explosion so that the two un-recovered may have been killed even if they had been a considerable distance away at the time of the first explosion.

The American dead were removed to their homes in the colliery ambulance as were some of the Italian victims, while others of the foreign workmen were removed to the undertaking establishment of J. Fred Dreisigacker. The bodies which were mangled by the explosion were taken to the undertaking parlors and prepared for burial. The five unidentified dead were removed to this establishment from the colliery office late in the evening.

DEATH IN THE MINES

Arrangements have been made for the burial of seven of them on Wednesday, all from one church. Contractor Portland has made arrangements to bear expense of the funerals of his workmen. Undertaker Bergen of Pottsville arrived Saturday night to prepare the remains of Daniel McGinley for burial.

The work of rescue by the second force [that] went into the mine was in [the] charge of Archbald McDonald, outside foreman who found about 10 men at his command, with an unlimited number of additional hands ready in the event of being needed.

The foremen from various collieries in the west end of the county also responded when they learned of the accident so there was no dearth of expert mining brains to conduct the rescue work. Besides Gen. Manager Richards, Supt. Kaercher, there were on hand P.F. Brenann, mining superintendent of the C. & I. Co., mine Inspector Price, Chief Engineer Mike Doyle, Outside Supt. Joseph Lee and others. From Otto, Lincoln, Good Springs and John Veith the bosses were on hand.

The wife of Thomas Behney was in Pottsville shopping Saturday and she was not aware of the accident until after the "Republican" appeared on the streets containing an excellent account of the accident in spite of the locality being very inaccessible. She was prostrated when she learned that her husband was among the dead.

Mrs. Hand, whose husband died just recently and the mother of the two Hand boys, who were killed, was also visiting Pottsville. She was the guest of Charles Riegel, deputy warden of the prison and she was informed by Mrs. Riegel that there had been an accident and one of her sons had been injured. She left at once for Muir, or Reiner City and the news was broken gently to her. She was prostrated with grief Saturday night and her friends were alarmed over her condition. The Hand boys were very popular throughout the entire valley. They were the support of their mother. Both of the Hand boys were expert ball players and their team was scheduled to play Saturday afternoon. For this reason Howard quit early and was about to leave the colliery for his home when the first explosion occurred and he hurried back into the mine with the rescuing force and met his death. Harry Hand also played on the same team.

The scene at the mouth of the slope was a tense one and although there were hundreds of men about from the different sections of the county there was scarcely a whisper. The men sat around the mouth on railroad ties and timber that had been pushed to the

The crew that sunk the shaft at the East Brookside Colliery down to a depth of 1,980 feet. *Courtesy of the Historical Society of Schuylkill County.*

scene and talked so quietly that one had to lean down to catch their words. There were hardly any women remained at the slope and only one or two girls from nearby towns were present, the mothers and daughters having gone to their homes when every ray of hope was gone.

All of the interest centered in the great sheave wheel which gave only a token of any movement in the mines. Occasionally it would move several feet and then a whisper would pass along, "They are coming up." Perhaps, it would stop and what the men were doing would be conveyed by the words "Another level." When the wheels would revolve slowly several times and then as the engine gathered speed start to wind the rope yard after yard the men would rise to their feet and gather about the rope that blocked off the entrance to the slope, peer anxiously into the depths for some sign of the missing men and then when nothing but corps were taken off the car would turn and walk slowly back to their seats.

When the relief corps were changed the men crowded forward to get on the car. The foreman found it so difficult to pick the men from the crowd that finally a list was made up previous to the cars coming up and as the next shift was called out. Only single men were taken and the older and married men were vexed because they were not given a chance. One man pressed forward and asked anxiously, "Are you looking for some one?" in hopes that he would be picked to go down. The boss replied "we want young fellows," and he got the half angry reply "I don't care, I am here to go down." These kind of dialogues were the ones that showed what the Schuylkill County miners are made of and there were more heroes of mine accidents in the group than Carnage will ever hear of. They did their duty with out any expectation of ever being given any reward. There were men in the group who have crawled down sluices to get injured workmen out and men that worked with rock falling all around them but they will never be known unless their butties give the stories of their heroism.

The mouth of the slope looked like a hospital. Ranged in lines were stretchers upon stretchers together with all of the paraphernalia and medicine of the first aid squads while two doctors stayed constantly on duty. But there was no need of any doctors and the only portion of the apparatus that was used was yard upon yard of linen that was needed to wrap the seared and broken bodies of the men before they were taken down the mountain.

As darkness gradually came on the scene the mountain became dotted with miners lamps as they paced to and fro from different sections of the workings. As the darkness became deeper and deeper they gathered in groups and went down the mountain hoping against hope that something would be heard soon.

According to one of the veteran miners at Tower City the men at that place died while taking precautions. When the accident occurred which wiped out the rescue party they were on their way by an indirect route, according to the men. The accidents which killed the foreigners [occurred] in the tunnel being driven by Portland people, off what is known as the big vein and is situated at the end of the number five gangway. The men when they went down instead of going in No. 5 went down the slope to No. 4 and then went out No. 4 to the lift. They then took the route upwards and when they struck the junction of No. 5 and the tunnel the accident occurred. The pocket of gas must have formed at this point after the explosion and the relief party evidently found no gas along the gangway until they ran into the pocket.

When the explosion occurred the terrible nature of the catastrophe became known there was no scarcity of volunteers. The men residing in the valley offered themselves as volunteers to go in and get their comrades out and the officials had a hard time to pick them. The first rescue corps to go down into the mine after the second explosion was that of the regular relief corps but after their return to the surface the experienced miners were picked. No thought of home or family was tolerated by the men and it made no difference what their position was. If they were needed they were there to do what was to be done. Many of the men worked without food from 11:00 o'clock in the morning until after eight at night and it was when all but the two missing were out that some thought was given of bodily needs. The officials at that time sent down to Reinerton for supplies and the men were given a light lunch. A number of the residents of the village made up baskets and cans and sent them up to the workings to the men and they were generously shared with all who were in need of food.

All of the relief corps from the nearby collieries were summoned as soon as the accident happened and they were the men who got the majority of the bodies out. The Lincoln corps together with those from John Veith, Lykens, Williamstown, Good Springs and the other collieries were on duty.

Harry Kimmel of the Lincoln Corps was one of the men who helped get the dead out and he stated that the scene in the slope was a terrible one. Men were lying about the gangway terribly battered and mangled while piles of rock and other debris made the rescue work difficult. He stated that although the majority of the men were killed by the force of the explosion and the deadly afterdamp was responsible for the deaths of quite a number. He gave as a reason for this that some of the bodies were but little bruised which denoted that they had fallen over when the deadly gas struck them. This was also the opinion of a number of other men who were in the mine. One of the chief troubles experienced by the men was that of falling roofs and sides. Falling rock made traveling difficult and the men who rescued Superintendent Lorenz were turned back from this cause.

Supt. Lorenz when found was carried by the men toward the mouth of the slope but on the way the danger from falling rock became so bad that they were obliged to take a circuitous route which finally carried them to the bottom of the shaft. The manner in which he was brought out according to the miners aquatinted with the workings caused the relief corps to carry the injured superintendent at least two miles. Big Jack Farrell the man whom he sent the rescuers after was carried the same distance. After his heroic words the Superintendent spoke a little of Farrell and those who carried him out state that after they passed Farrell's body which was being carried by other members of the corps that he did not mention his name and it is the opinion that Lorenz realized his comrade was dead.

The Draeger Helmets were used by the relief men and they proved to be of inestimable value. The helmets are of recent invention on the order of a fireman helmet and supply air independent of any outside ventilation for three hours. The helmet is of a rubber construction which is placed over the head and then made air proof by an automatic attachment. A plate glass in the front gives the operator plenty of view. The air is supplied by a tank which is fastened to the operators back and contains a purifying device. The air is then fed to the man using it by a rubber tube. The supply lasts for three hours and the amount used is registered by a dial on the front. When the helmet has been used for two hours and a half the dial points to danger on the glass and the operator is then required to return to get a fresh supply.

Considerable excitement was occasioned in Reinerton shortly after nine o'clock, when the bodies of the five Tyroleans who were killed were brought down the mountain. The bodies were brought down, wrapped in sheets and two were placed in a wagon, the undertaking facilities being so meager that it was necessary to bring them down in spring wagons. As the teams drove silently around the corner the people crowded the curb to look and then turned away sickened by the gruesome sight.

An ominous sign was given out when one of the relief corps came up and shortly after eight o'clock reported that hundreds of tons of rock and a big pocket of gas was barring their further progress. This cut out the work from the one side of the fatal spot and after that the squad on duty worked from the other side. It took considerable time to reach the spot and when word was received that they arrived on the scene the men would be notified by one of their number who remained constantly near the telephone. This was the only word received from below.

A peculiar feature of the explosion was the fact that the mules that were in the workings were not killed and only slightly injured. This was commented upon by the men and they could give no cause. That the mules escaped the concussion of the explosion and the after damp also is one of the peculiar things that hangs about all accidents and is never explained.

One of the most fortunate men in the region was Hillary Zimmerman, who according to two stories about the mouth of the slope was the only man in the mine at the time of the explosion to escape unscathed. Zimmerman according to the miners was at the bottom of the slope when the explosion occurred and was knocked ten feet by the concussion. He was picked up by the rescue group in a badly stunned condition but rapidly recovered, being able to return to the colliery shortly afterward and assist in the work.

Nothing is being overlooked in an effort to save Harry Schoffstall, the only survivor. He is so terribly burned that it would seem he had no chance to get well but Dr. Hawk and the two trained nurses attending him are doing everything within their power and they doggedly declare there is hope to save him.

A hull of iron spikes did deadly execution among the men according to Mr. Colbert, and this is borne out by the undertakers. Mr. Colbert stated that there were several kegs of hook spikes, better known as railroad spikes in the gangway when the explosion occurred and that the dynamite sent them hurling on their deadly course. Several of the men taken out had spikes in their bodies and here and there in the debris and at several hundred feet spikes have been picked up. No wonder the men are dead. They not only had concussion and fire to go through but were met by a rain of iron which no human body could withstand.

The Funerals

Although the scenes at the American homes are sad, those at the Italian homesteads are far worse. The American wives have the consolation and help of neighbors, but the Italian women have their dead lying in the homes with no one able to help them because of the fact they cannot understand English. Many of the houses have many boarders and they are standing around helpless to aid the afflicted. A pitiful scene took place in Muir on Monday evening. One of the Italians who was killed was badly mangled, and when the undertaker got his mangled body in a condition when it could be viewed his wife was led in to see him. It was the first the woman had seen her husband since he left for work on Saturday morning and alive and hearty, and the poor woman collapsed under the strain. She was carried into a neighbor's house and the men, helpless to aid her, stood half dazed by the scene.

One little girl, aged 13, the oldest of the three, went about one of the homes heartbroken and sick endeavoring to do what little work was to be done while her mother lay in the parlor, prostrated by the tragedy.

Another wife walked in a half dazed condition down the yard and up again in what seemed to be a never ending walk with one baby toddling by her side and another in her arms. She herself is soon to become a mother and the residents say "It is such scenes as these that is casting a spell over the valley, and with no way that the sadness can be alleviated the situation is one of a dejected helplessness."

There will be eight funerals of the mine victims held Wednesday, seven of them at Tower City and one at Tremont, that of Supt. Lorenz.

There are not enough hearses in the Williams Valley to provide for the Tower City funerals, although they have been borrowed from every available source. Five hearses have been secured and it has been arranged to remove two of the bodies to the church and then the hearses return to the houses of the dead and all five will arrive at the church at the same time on the second trip. After the services five bodies will be taken to the cemetery.

Solemn requiem high mass was celebrated in St. Peter and St. Paul Catholic Church at nine o'clock Tuesday morning over the remains of John Farrell, Daniel McGinley and Henry Murphy. The remains were brought to the church in three hearses and the caskets were arranged near the altar. The church was crowded with the families and with relatives and friends of the deceased colliery bosses. Outside were hundreds who were unable to gain admittance but who stood silently and with every indication of grief during the entire funeral service. A dozen priests were present and participated in the mass, which was the most solemn and impressive ever performed in the county. Rev. Vincent Corcoran, of Lost Creek, was celebrant of the mass. Rev. Francis Ward, of New Philadelphia the deacon.

After the conclusion of the very impressive service, the caskets were carried from the edifice by stalwart miners and close friends of the deceased who acted as pall bearers. The remains of Foreman John Farrell were taken by trolley to Williamstown where interment was made in the catholic cemetery. The funeral cortege of Daniel McGinley moved to the railroad station, from where the train proceeded to New Philadelphia and interment was made in the Holy Family cemetery. The funeral of Henry Murphy proceeded to the parish cemetery of the Church of the Immaculate Conception at Tremont. Thomas Behney, of Reinerton was laid to rest in the beautiful little Orwin cemetery Tuesday morning. Employees from the colliery attended the funeral in a body and the pall bearers were fellow workmen. The remains were in an oak casket. Hundreds visited the house before the service to see the remains and pay tribute to his memory and offer a word of sympathy and consolation to the family.

The East Brookside Colliery, "Explosion!"

The funeral of Jacob Kopenhaver was also held on Tuesday morning and interment was made in the Lutheran Reformed cemetery. As was the case at the other funerals there was a large delegation of miners present and the pall bearers were selected from their number.

Preparations were made Monday evening for the removal of the bodies of Victoria Zonanuri the blacksmith and Egidio Tucki to Hazelton on Tuesday by the Pennsylvania train. Interment was made in the Tyrolean cemetery.

Alec Linshnit, the boarding boss where the above two men and Carrinna Dreanipi boarded will be buried Wednesday at Tower City. Linshnit has a wife and three children. Linshnit was one of the most prominent Italians in that section and was well liked. He was a powerful man and of handsome appearance. His death wipes out one of the best friends of the aliens in that district.

Mrs. Linshnit, wife of the boarding boss is making preparations to return to the old country with her family. She has relations in Italy and America holds no attraction for her since her husband lost his life. The one girl Anna the oldest is opposed to the plan. Mrs. Koppenhaver, and family will go to Orwin where they will make their home with her parents. The Hand family will continue in their home at Muir.

The Hand boys, Howard and Harry were buried on Tuesday morning from their homes at Muir, interment being made in the Fairview Cemetery at Orwin. Numerous floral offerings were sent to the home Monday evening, among which was a handsome tribute from the Tower City Cubs, the base ball team to which the men belonged. The boys were conveyed to the cemetery by two hearses and laid side by side in the family plot.

At the hotel of Jops. Kusputis of Reinerton, the bodies of four of the Italian workmen have been laid out in one of the rooms. The fifth, that of the mucker boss, Carinna Dreanipi was taken to the place on Tuesday evening from the Linshnit home. The four Italians at the Kusputis home are Antonio Apaschi, Nick Difoudope, and Riccardo Twedanzi. All of the above men were in Muir but a short time and were practically unknown. They will be buried in the Peter's Mountain cemetery.

August 8, 1913 the search for the missing men Fessler and Farley continued. Additional impetus was given to the search for Messrs. Fessler and Farley at E. Brookside on Thursday evening when the rescue party ran into an open space of 20 feet, after having made poor progress all day. The opening places the party within 15 feet of the supposed dynamite explosion and the men have every reason to

believe that the bodies will be recovered either tonight or Saturday with
a chance of their being uncovered on Friday afternoon. Ever since the
explosion the men worked with a possibility of discovering the bodies
of the men every minute and this proposition still holds good.

This piece of good fortune started the men at work with
redoubled energy and they are now hoping that a few hours work
will disclose another space. The open space saved at least two days
digging and makes the discovery of the bodies that much earlier.

Harry Schoffstall, the sole survivor of the explosion is improving
rapidly and his chance of recovery is said to be excellent. He was
in the best condition Thursday evening than at any time since the
explosion and although terribly burned may escape by a slender
thread the fate of his comrades in the mine.

On Saturday, August 9, the county was shocked by the news that Harry
Schoffstall had died at his home in Orwin. Schoffstall, who was the assistant fire
boss, was in the mine at the time of the first explosion but was nearer to the slope
and a safe distance away when the first explosion occurred. He then went with the
rescuing party to the aid of the Italian workmen and was caught in the second
explosion and severely burned. He was thirty-two years old at the time of his death.

Mr. Schoffstall was a particularly unfortunate miner he having figured
in two previous accidents the past year in addition to the one which
caused his death. He was terribly burned about the body by the
explosion and the only spot where he wasn't burned was where his
shirt had rolled inside of his trousers. He was able to give a partial
account of the accident to his father but was unconscious when
taken out of the mine and was unable to give an account outside of
the explosion and his crawling several feet.

Mr. Schoffstall was given the best care by Dr. Hawk, and two
trained nurses in addition to his father being constantly at his
bedside. Although small hope was held for his recovery at the time
of the accident he rallied during the week and was admitted to
having a fighting chance. However he grew weaker Friday evening
and passed away this morning. Mr. Schoffstall was married to a miss
Margaret Hand of Orwin and is a very distant relation to the Hand
boys who lost their lives. Two children besides his wife survive.

In speaking of the death of Harry Schoffstall, his sister, Mrs.
Jacob Linn, of Tremont, says that since the accident one week ago,

THE EAST BROOKSIDE COLLIERY, "EXPLOSION!"

Harry suffered untold agony, his terrible burns on the arms and body exuding blood matter, occasioning the changing of bandages frequently at which times his cries were most heartrending. Mrs. Linn assisted the injured man's wife, who has remained at his bedside since the accident of one week ago, and knowing the suffering he has gone through the past week they are reconciled to the fact, as there appeared to be no hope for his entire recovery. He is now relieved of longer agony. He was a patient sufferer, but there seemed to be no chance for him, for, besides the indescribable burns he had a bruise on the side of his head that in itself would be almost a fatal one.

With a week passed since the terrible accident at the E. Brookside colliery the mystery of the explosion was nearer a solution on Saturday than it had been for any time during the week. Fourteen feet were uncovered by the rescue party on Friday night and 29 feet uncovered on Saturday. This has thrown the workers within a few feet of the site where the dynamite was and whether it was dynamite or gas in the first explosion will be solved tonight or Sunday. It is extremely probable that Sunday morning will see this portion of the mystery solved and the bodies of the men recovered.

An indication of the proximity of the spot was obtained Friday when the battery used to fire the charges of dynamite was recovered together with several safety lamps. The lamps are all of the type used by the miners however, and one of the fire boss lamps which is different in shape has been recovered. The large force of workmen engaged in clearing the gangway have brought conclusive evidence that there are dead bodies within early reaching distance as decomposition has set in and it has been found necessary to adopt measures in an effort to purify the air. While there is a possibility that the odor may come from the bodies of the mules it is the general impression that the bodies of the two missing fire bosses will be found before the passing of the day.

The question has been raised whether this was the worst mine accident in the history of the county. A former St. Clair and Wadesville resident who says that he remembers about 40 years ago of an accident in the old Wadesville shaft when it was an individual operation, of an explosion occurring which resulted in the death of 23. Others who were residents of St. Clair at that time had no recollection of such an accident when the matter was broached.

The Headlines read, "Dynamite Not The Cause of The Tower City Disaster." The explosion at the East Brookside mine which

DEATH IN THE MINES

Top: A group of miners gets instructions from the boss before going to their work area. Notice how they are all carrying safety lamps. *Courtesy of the author.*

Left: The underground hospital built into the rock wall at the East Brookside Colliery where the explosion on August 2, 1913, took twenty lives. *Courtesy of the Historical Society of Schuylkill County.*

resulted in the death of 20 men August 2, was not caused by dynamite but more probably by gas was indicated by the finding Sunday of the dynamite intact which had been taken into the mine on the morning of the explosion.

The residents of Tower City are all at sea regarding the cause of the explosion as a result of the discovery of the dynamite and the theory of a dynamite explosion followed by a gas one has been abandoned altogether. According to one of the prominent men at that place it is now up to the inquest, and if the investigation cannot solve the mystery then the cause of the explosion will never be known.

The amount of dynamite in the mine was fixed by Supt. Lorenz in his dying statement as six boxes or 150 pounds but the men placed the amount at seven boxes. The latter was the amount of boxes found and the sticks were lying in the gangway where they were placed by the men after being taken out of the boxes. The boxes in which the dynamite was packed were found as well as the tools and the box detonators which were used to fire the explosive. All of the materials found point conclusively to the fact that the explosion was not one of dynamite.

No trace of the bodies of Fessler and Farley has been found by the men at work and the finding of the dynamite has banished their strong hopes of finding the men. It was supposed that the men would be in the immediate vicinity of where the dynamite was, but no trace of them has been found. The odor which was discernible on Saturday and was supposed to come from the bodies decomposing was caused by dead rats which were found in the gangway. The only theory now as to where the bodies are located is that they are in the air shaft, which has not been cleared, and the work of clearing it will be rushed, so as to allow the men to work from both sides. The P & R. Company has only hired single men for the rescue work so hazardous is the task of clearing the debris away and the men hired are being paid wages of $4.00 a day for their services.

In an effort to determine the cause of the deadly accident that killed twenty men at the East Brookside Colliery an inquest was held, beginning on Tuesday, August 12, 1913. The inquest was conducted by Coroner Moore and assisted by Deputy Coroner Phillips. Another prominent member of the inquest was Mine Inspector Price. A lengthy investigation was expected, with many witnesses being called, including colliery officials, the first aid corps of the colliery, members of the rescue gang and the lamp man, a crucial witness. One of the most sensational parts of the inquest occurred when Charles Hand, of Reiner City, testified that the company did not observe safety rules requiring safety lamps to be locked. Mr. Hand was the lamp man at East Brookside. Following are some extracts from the coroner's inquest.

Charles Hand who had charge of the safety lamps said that the men who went into the mine that day had safety lamps and that the lamps recovered were all battered up. He said he delivered the lamps to the men every day without being locked. He said he had never been instructed to lock them. He is acquainted with the law relative to the use of these lamps and he did not consider it necessary to use safety lamps in all parts of the mine.

Juror Henry had in his possession a copy of the mining laws and read the extract with references to the use of safety lamps. They are required in all mines where gas is known to exist in dangerous quantities. He asked if there was any one who could testify to the condition of the East Brookside workings which would give the jury the opportunity to judge whether safety lamps were necessary for use always in the mine. It was suggested that no man was better qualified on this subject than Mine Inspector Price and he was called.

Mr. Price stated that he had made an inspection of the mine Wednesday preceding that tragic Saturday and that he had gone through the mine with a naked lamp. He considered it safe or he would not have risked his own life by carrying a naked lamp into dangerous places. He said he had talked to Farley in reference to his district, it was in his district were the explosion occurred, and he had been assured that everything was all right and there was no work being done which necessitated any inspection of an unusual character. He said he examined the books of the fire bosses and found nothing unusual. He also testified that he had a copy of a report by mine foreman Farrell in which a sworn statement was made that there was no new work being done which necessitated any inspection because the men never worked in such places.

The explosion which occurred in this mine August 2 was an unusual circumstance which could not be foreseen by any. These men who came to their deaths were better able to see it than anyone and yet [that] they walked to their deaths indicated they had no fear of anything of this kind happening. He considered East Brookside a safe mine as far as gas was concerned and did not consider the use of safety lamps at all times necessary.

On August 14, 1913, the *Pottsville Daily Republican* ran an article on what they surmised the theory of the explosion would be:

After careful consideration of opinions of leading miners in the Williams Valley, it is being generally accepted and again it is probable that Coroner Moore will work along corresponding lines at the hearing on Monday next. Coroner Moore has narrowed the cause to two theories although the one is based partly upon the first one which is the one advanced by the *Republican* on Wednesday evening.

The theory now generally accepted is that a fall or rush occurred in the gangway and that the cloud of dust seen in the fan house was caused by the in rush of air. This naturally made some commotion and at the same time released a large pocket of gas. The report of this rush caused the rescue party to be formed and at the same time alarmed Supt. Lorenz, Farrell, McGinley, Fessler and Farley fire bosses who were in the mine together with the Italian laborers in the tunnel. This caused all of the above to start for the probable scene. The Italians sticking their shovels in the debris and starting for the mouth of the tunnel. In the meantime the rescue party and the bosses were making in the same direction. What caused the second explosion is not known from the evidence but it is generally conceded that one of the three parties [of] above named men were to blame. The Italian laborers without their carbide lights may have been the cause, the coroner eliminating the rescue men because they had safety lamps. Farley or Fessler who have not been found yet may have caused it; finding their remains may have a lot to do with solving this mystery.

The second theory is identical with the above with the exception that instead of a rush of coal the Italians may have caused a small explosion which released a large pocket of gas which was fired from something burning from the first explosion.

The above theory is not Dr. Moores but is built up after his views had been obtained together with those of prominent mining men and the facts adduced from the evidence. The only thing unexplained had been the lack of fire and this is to be believed to be due to the fact that the vacuum created by the explosion was so great that the resulting inrush of air put everything that showed a sign of fire out. It is more than likely that the hearing of Monday will be carried upon these lines.

In the early morning of Friday August 15, Daniel Farley's body was found in the debris of the fall which was caused by the explosion and was in a good state of preservation. The body was pinned on a fall of rock and coal which reached to the waist and was badly burned. After being taken out and dressed the mans remains were taken to his home in Tower City.

The Coroner was seen this morning regarding the finding of Farley's body and he stated that he believed that the finding would throw some light on the cause although he had received no details yet.

The East Brookside mine gave up the last of its victims on Friday evening at ten o'clock when the rescue party recovered the body of the fire boss John Fessler. Fessler's body was found face forward with a covering of dirt and rock completely hiding it. It was approximately eleven feet away from the spot where Daniel Farley the victim found Friday morning was lying. The body was immediately placed in a hermetically sealed casket and removed to the Fessler homestead in Tower City. The discovery of Fessler's body closes another chapter in the history of the mine disaster and the men who have been working frantically for the past thirteen days have now concluded their task.

According to the talk of the men who were working the finding of the bodies has no tendency to throw a light on the cause of the explosion and all hope that the bodies of the men would give some clue to the cause have been shattered and the mystery is apparently as deep as ever.

The colliery may resume work on Tuesday, according to the statement of the men. West Brookside has been working for the past three days and all is in readiness to start E. Brookside. The colliery according to witnesses at the inquest was very little damaged outside of the immediate vicinity of the explosion. Reports from Tower City state that many of the men will be missing when the colliery starts as a number of the miners have expressed themselves as being through with the place.

On August 20, 1913, the finding of the coroner's inquest was presented to the public with the following verdict rendered:

We find that the said 18 men came to their deaths as a result of an explosion of gas in Fire boss Daniel Farley's district, but from the evidence we fail to find that it was caused by negligence of the company or contributory negligence on the part of anyone.

The inquest of Farley and Fessler was held on Friday and the conclusion was the same as the previous inquest. So the final chapter of the most fearful accident that ever happened in the anthracite coal mining region of Schuylkill County came to an end.

LYTLE MINE
"A DEADLY EXPLOSION
OF GAS"
PRIMROSE, PENNSYLVANIA
SEPTEMBER 24, 1943

World War II was in its second year and news from the war highlighted most of the headlines. There hadn't been a major mine accident in five years. At 1:30 p.m. on September 24, 1943, a deadly explosion of gas occurred in the Moffet and Schrader Coal Company Mine in Primrose, Pennsylvania, better known by its old name, the Lytle.

The Lytle Mine was an old one. It had been worked since the late 1880s, when it was owned by the Susquehanna Coal Company. A number of lesser gas explosions took a toll of lives in the mine during the 1920s. After a few years the mine became a cooperative venture of the miners, operating under the name of the Primrose Coal Company. By the 1940s it was known as the M&S Coal Company. J.M. Farley was the general manager. It was a dangerous mine. For many years miners dug coal in its veins and many were hurt working in its gangways and chutes. In 1892, ten miners were drowned when an inrush of water came in on them from an old working. Then in 1905, five men were killed when the roof collapsed. By 1943 the mine employed over three hundred men, including the breaker and outside workers. At the time of the accident the men were working over one thousand feet below the surface. Once again the Lytle would take its toll, this time with the lives of fourteen men.

A view of the head frame at the Lytle Coal Company used for hoisting the cars from the slope. Also pictured is the engine house and pump house that provides the steam. *Courtesy of the author.*

This is the head frame of the Lytle Colliery near Minersville where the September 24, 1943 explosion took many lives. *Courtesy of the author.*

Lytle Mine, "A Deadly Explosion of Gas"

The *Pottsville Republican* reported on the tragedy.

The day shift was nearly over for the men working in the mechanical loading section north of the barrier on the fifth level of the old Lytle mine. The fifth level was a little over 1,000 feet below the surface. The explosion took place about 4,000 feet from the bottom of the shaft at the extreme end of the workings in a large area covering some 1500 square feet. The crew consisted of Nicholas Stanko, Robert Thompson, John Adams, Ernest Truscott, Tony Yepcavage, Bernard "Barney" Mileshosky, Ronald Brown, Albert Narres, Andrew Kamykowski, John DiBiase, Robert Edwards, George Bobrick, John Dando, and Albert Levashouskas all residing in Minersville. August Felli and Arch Miller, Pottsville. John Pielacha, George Tracey, and Steve Keitsock, Forrestville. Michael Liptock, Primrose. Lester Klingler, Wisconisco and James Connelly filled out the ranks of day shift miners.

According to the inspectors, the explosion was ignited from an unknown origin, most likely a spark from some equipment. After the explosion occurred the less seriously hurt were given treatment at the mine or rushed to the Warne Hospital in Pottsville and given treatment. Immediately word spread throughout the area, rescue crews from local collieries all volunteered their services for a rescue attempt and rushed to the mine. Their services were not needed at this time because of an accumulation of poisons' gas and the victims could not be brought to the surface. It was realized that those who were still trapped were dead.

At first it was thought that an accumulation of dust caused the accident, but State Secretary of the Mines, Richard Maize claimed dust played no part in it. He explained that a condition like this may have existed had the explosion taken place in a bituminous operation where the mines are extremely dusty. Mr. Maize stated that "Until the air in the mine has been cleared of deadly gas and the bodies are recovered the operation will be closed pending a state investigation." The order effected nearly all the workers at the colliery and stopped the mining of over a 1,000 tons of coal mined.

The explosion occurred in the area where the coal was being loaded onto cars being pulled by electric motors. The force of the explosion knocked out stoppings, which are used to expedite ventilation, and parts of the "top," halting ventilation in the mechanical loading section and caused undetermined damage to the loading equipment in that section.

DEATH IN THE MINES

An overhead electric motor used to haul cars in and out of the mine. The electric motor replaced the mule for haulage methods. *Courtesy of the author.*

Finally it was safe for rescuers to enter and rescue workers worked feverishly to reach the trapped miners on the afternoon of September 24, but by 10:00 P.M. only four bodies were brought to the surface. The rescuers reported that they had to leave ten other bodies underground. According to the rescuers seven of the ten were identified, but three were so badly burned from the effects of the explosion that they could not be identified.

Late that evening Inspector Maize ordered the rescue work halted because of the After Damp which endangered the lives of the rescuers. A fan to expel the deadly gas was installed at 4 A.M. Saturday after a motor to operate it arrived from Scranton. Gradually the level was cleared of the dreaded After Damp.

By early Saturday afternoon the mine was deemed safe enough to enter again to recover the bodies. Miners from the Mahanoy City Colliery Rescue team were the first to enter the explosion area. They reported that many of the victims were found badly burned, some with the clothing burned from them. Some were in grotesque crouched positions where they died from the deadly fumes. According to them, no bodies were blasted or dismembered.

When the word reached the families of the victims that they had all been found the family members all rushed to the top of the shaft. There

In this photograph a miner is given first aid by his fellow miners before being removed to the surface. *Courtesy of the author.*

many women became hysterical. Ropes were stretched around the top of the shaft and Pennsylvania State Police were there to maintain order.

All of the victims were identified at the bottom of the shaft by the rescue workers, some of whom were buddies of the victims. The rescuers attached slips of paper with the men's names written on them and attached them to the blankets that covered them. Two at a time the bodies were brought to the surface and the first bodies to reach the top were those of Al Leveshauskas and John Adams of Minersville.

A girlfriend of Leveshauskas who was in the crowd of spectators was seen sobbing openly. She almost collapsed as the stretcher bearing his body passed her. The two were to have been married.

As more of the bodies came to the surface, the crowd became hushed. The only sound was that of mournful sobbing of the women and the children.

Residents of Primrose who lived near the mine were badly shaken by the loss of life in this accident. But most who had family members working in the mine expressed great relief that the explosion didn't take place when the second shift would have been entering the mine. Most feared more lives would have been lost.

Sometimes fate can play a part in a disaster. It seems fate saved the lives of two men who may normally have been in the area

DEATH IN THE MINES

Miners load an injured man onto a stretcher for removal to the surface. *Courtesy of the Historical Society of Schuylkill County.*

where the explosion took place. Thomas Reilly of Primrose, who was supposed to work on the day shift had exchanged work shift with his friend John Dando, who met his death in the explosion. John MacDonald of Primrose was injured earlier and by fortune did not report to work as a repairman on this day.

Robert Miller, a foreman at Lytle was saved because a miner asked him to get a new light for his lamp. Within two minutes of leaving to get the light the explosion occurred. Robert was knocked down by the force of the explosion and was unconscious when found. Robert's father, Archibald Miller, was not so fortunate. He was killed in the blast.

Another odd story that surrounds this tragedy was that of Robert Edwards who was driving home on Thursday night with his brother Samuel, Chief of Police in Minersville. They came upon an automobile accident in which a woman was instantly killed. The two brothers talked of the tragedy they just witnessed with no thought that Robert would meet a violent death the next day in the "Old Lytle."

3.
CAVE-INS, ROOF COLLAPSE, INRUSH OF WATER

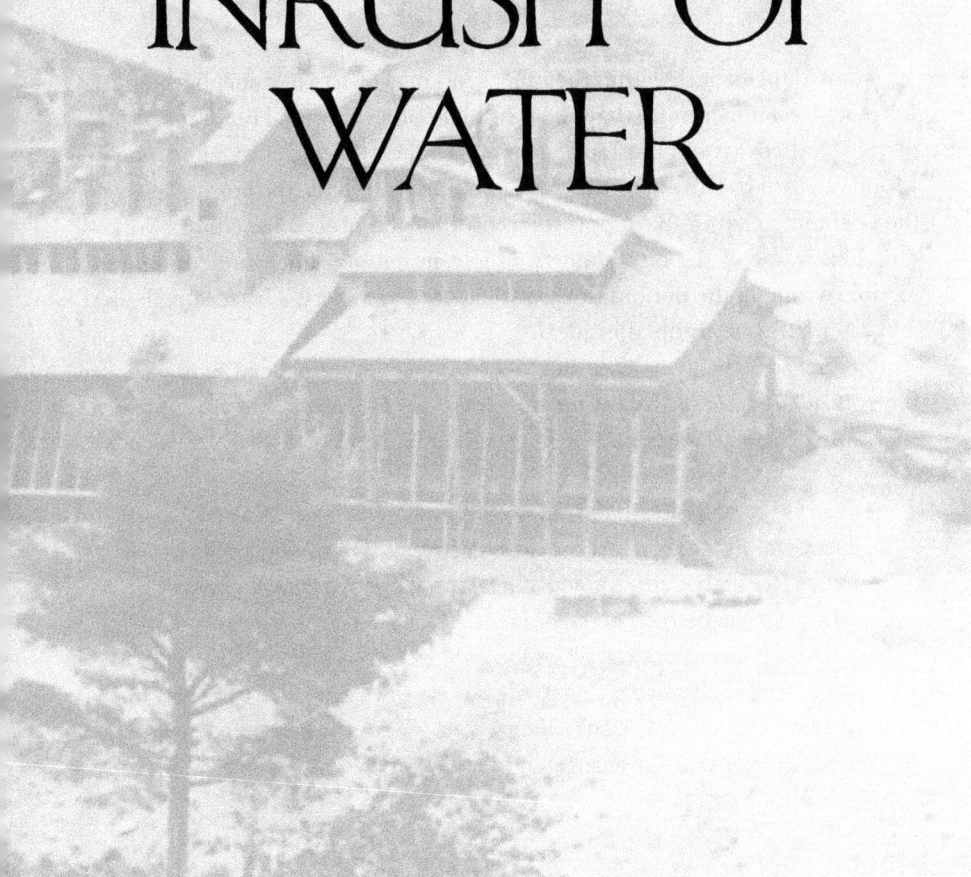

CUYLER COLLIERY "BURIED ALIVE"

RAVEN RUN, PENNSYLVANIA

APRIL 6, 1885

M any dangers lurk within the inner workings of a coal mine, but nothing scares a miner more than the possibility of a roof fall. Hundreds of tons of rock and coal could crush or entrap the miner. On the early afternoon of Monday, April 6, 1885, ten men were robbing the pillars, the cutting away of the coal that is left in to support the roof after the breasts have been worked out. This is one of the most dangerous jobs in mining. Then something went terribly wrong in the bottom slope of the Cuyler Colliery. The roof collapsed and ten men were trapped inside.

The first reports of the cave-in reached the general public at 5:30 p.m. via the *Pottsville Republican*. Following the story, the *Republican* sent a reporter to the scene of the accident and began sending back reports.

> Cuyler colliery, situated at Raven Run, was the scene of a terrible accident yesterday afternoon. Two men who were working inside were literally buried alive, and at this writing it is not known whether the men can be rescued or not.
>
> About one o'clock a fall of the top rock several hundred yards in extent, took place shutting in Mike Harrity, Henry Mervine, Ben Mauer, Nick Purcell, Daniel Kenny, John Anderson and son, Frank McLaughlin, John Cavanaugh and Barney Smith; the five first listed

CUYLER COLLIERY, "BURIED ALIVE"

One of the dangers of a working mine, the fall of the roof. Here a miner is trapped under the debris. *Courtesy of the author.*

are married and all are residents of Raven Run. The colliery is an old one and will be worked out in a few months.

For some time past they have been robbing the place out and, the interior is nothing but a shell. Not even the stumps of pillars was [sic] allowed to stand and the disaster that happened yesterday had been expected for some time but not with such terrible results. Some of the men refused to work and returned to their homes, but as miners say good money is made by such work, and without much trouble nothing could persuade the others to quit work. There are five lifts on the slope and the cave in extended from the surface to the number five lift. The two Andersons and Frank McLaughlin are shut in No. 2, while the others are in No. 4, two lifts below. Many narrow escapes were made, some of them within an ace of losing their lives. All afternoon every effort was made to find a loop hole to rescue the imprisoned men but they were futile. Rescuing parties would first try one way then another, but their hopes dwindled to nothing towards evening. The news of the accident was soon spread about the neighboring country and in a few hours the place was crowded. About the mines and in the patches where the men live the scenes beggared description. The families of the unfortunate men were grief stricken and were all hoping against hope that their fathers and brothers could be recovered either dead or alive.

Here a miner stands next to a pillar of coal. The pillar was left in to support the roof. *Courtesy of the author.*

A mule is lowered down the shaft. Notice how he is harnessed with his halter fastened to the frame so he can't move about. *Courtesy of the author.*

Cuyler Colliery, "Buried Alive"

The latest reports from the scene of the disaster are to the effect that the bodies of two of the unfortunate men may be recovered by three months steady work, but the other eight are buried beyond the hope of ever getting them out.

Saturday April 11, 1885 there was no change in the work at Raven Run. On Thursday all work of rescuing the entombed men was stopped, those in charge deeming it advisable. Should the fall come that is expected, those who know say they can never recover the bodies of some of them. It is not known how long work will be suspended.

A relief fund has been started for the benefit of the sufferers from the accident, the following appeal was issued at a meeting on Friday. The caving in of the mines at Raven Run has brought desolation, sorrow and misery onto the families of the victims whose bodies are still buried in the closed in gangways. The wives and children of the dead men appeal to our sympathy and charity for consolation. They sit desolate in their homes waiting for the dead; but we can relieve the poverty in which these helpless ones are left. Six of the men left large helpless families, and at the present they are in want of the necessities of life. By relieving their poverty we will take away some of the bitterness of their grief.

On April 14, 1885, a correspondent of the *Shenandoah Herald* writing from the scene of the accident said:

The gloom and sorrow which has hung like a cloud over the inhabitants of this place for the past week still continues, but with more hope that something will soon be heard from inside the mine. When it was decided to abandon all searches several days ago, the news was heralded throughout the patches and soon reached the families of the imprisoned miners, producing such a scene of grief and lamentation as is seldom seen even in the coal regions.

Everything therefore reports to an early recovery of at least the three men in no. 2 lift. The excitement at the colliery has somewhat subsided. The large crowds of people who remained at and around the mouth of the mine has grown smaller. The work of timbering in no. 2 and 4 levels was resumed and carried on without any intermission on Friday night. The two mules which were found yesterday morning are still inside. Efforts, however, to get them out from the top of the fall where they now lie are being made. This step is necessary on account of the bad stench from decomposition. The stench from them somewhat retards the progress of the men. In the mean time chloride of lime in large quantities is being sent inside and used to counteract as much as possible. Several theories advanced as to how the mules met their death. One is that they were killed by the sudden shock or concussion of the air. The others that they were suffocated by after damp. They lay side by side, the head of one facing eastward, the other westward, neither of the mules have any marks, with the exception of a slight cut on the knee of one of them. The harnesses remain intact. How they reached the place where they were found is a singular feature of the case and can't be fully explained, there being only a few feet of space between the roof and their bodies. The greatest mystery in connection with the terrible accident and one which at present seems impossible to explain is what caused the great up heave of the bottom in No. 2 level, there being a solid mass of coal three hundred feet beneath it. A geologist's explanation will be received on the subject.

Three eight hour shifts with eight men on each are now hard at work and are making rapid headway in timbering in both levels. The mine settled to almost a perfect stillness and everything looks better for reaching the entombed men soon. In fact it has got down to a question of clearing and taking out the debris. Messrs. Heaton & Co. are making superhuman efforts to accomplish this but experience great difficulty in getting men to go inside. The miners employed at the colliery here are too deeply affected by the terrible fate of their companions, and while many of them are working the majority can not work. Mr. Robert Heston however, is doing all in his power to keep all the shifts full and employing miners wherever they can be found to assist. This morning two loaded wagons bearing the ticket of William Anderson in No. 2 level were found, and taken out. An empty wagon can also be seen on the same level, but cannot be reached yet. It is possible that the men in the level will be found inside of ten or fifteen hours if they were not blown up the breast by the concussion, in which case no one can tell when they will be rescued. Rapid headway is also being made on No. 4 level. Cheering reports come from that quarter and a better feeling prevails everywhere. Coal and Iron Policemen George Geiger and Peter Kreiger are on duty today and no one will be allowed to enter the mine.

The driver boy of the mines; an excellent study of a young boy and his cut plait whip. *Courtesy of Library of Congress.*

DEATH IN THE MINES

The company inspector checks the quality of the coal mined. *Courtesy of the author.*

On April 25, 1885, three weeks after the accident, the first of the bodies was recovered from the mine. The *Journal* reported that, although fearfully mangled and greatly decomposed, he was finally recognized as John Anderson, son of William Anderson, whose remains were still in the ill-fated mine.

> The authorities are keeping the matter very quiet in order to prevent any undue excitement. It is thought some of the other bodies in No. 2 lift in which the body was found will soon be reached.
>
> Three days later the body of the driver boy Frank Mclaughlin was found, his head was nearly severed from his body and the body was terribly mutilated. The following testimony was heard by the jury investigating this accident, the *Journal* would report the most important parts of the testimony.
>
> William H. Heston sworn; "I am superintendent of the colliery. I considered the colliery in first class condition; had made special efforts to keep it in that condition. Had a long flat slope, divided into four lifts; there was no premonition of the accident at all. The only intimation he had was four weeks ago, when the inside superintendent told him that he had ordered out the men on the second level, as the mine had commenced working. Main top rock broke, something that has

Cuyler Colliery, "Buried Alive"

been never known to happen before, so far as he could learn from the experience of mine superintendents. Did not know the men were on the second level. The men on the fourth level were sent to stand props. The men were sent in on the lower level by the inside boss, by my sanction. There was no indication of a crash on the fourth level. The trouble was on the second level. Considered the colliery perfectly safe; would have been willing to take my family in. My object in sending the men in the fourth lift was to make it more secure. The men on the fourth lift were experienced miners. Purcell had been at the colliery for nineteen years. Mardy had been with the colliery for nine years. They were accustomed to that sort of work, and worked on the place the previous Saturday. The Andersons had been working at the colliery for twelve years. Young Mclaughlin had been working at the colliery on and off for the past six years. The fall caught them at once. The extent of the fall was not definitely ascertained. It was thought to be about three hundred yards in a diagonal direction. The tremendous concussion on the water level was evidence the fall was sudden. In the fourth level the concussion sent the mules, which had taken timber to the men, to the front of the slope. The water level pitch runs on the outside about six degrees further in about fifteen degrees. A car was driven a considerable distance up the slope by the concussion. The force of miners had been augmented since the first of the year."

William Stein, Mine Inspector-elect, sworn; "I am inside foreman at Hammond colliery; was here after the accident; went in 400 feet in No. 2 and found it generally squeezing, I don't know all the conditions of the colliery sufficiently to say whether it would be safe or not to timber in No. 4. I did not visit any other parts of the mine except the gangway."

Mine Inspector Mauchline, sworn; "I was in the Cuyler colliery on the 12th of December last, inspected the place where James Cullen, on the second lift was killed at that time. Found the working in the usual condition. Didn't visit the colliery next until April 6th; I considered it only a matter of time until it would start to squeeze somewhere. I have general supervision of over five collieries; Knowing the colliery as I do I would not have left the miners to go in the fourth lift, when No. 2 lift was working heavily, when I went in it was working violently on the stumps, I did not anticipate a general fall; I don't think the fall came all at once; my theory is it must have worked very violently a few seconds, perhaps minutes before the crash; I think the miners must have been loading timber, or doing something that distracted their attention from the crash, as I think there must have been sufficient warning for them to run a considerable distance before the fall occurred in front of them. In the rush from the scene they may have been hemmed in from another fall. Their lights were likely blown out also, and the men were bewildered and did not know which way to go. From the hardness of the top and coal there must have been a fearful noise previous to the fall. The miners were aware that Mr. Edgar had kept them out of this place, and of course they must have gone in with the knowledge that there was danger, when I put the men to work after the fall, I thought I could detect any likelihood of another fall and get the men out in time. I think the men are now working in what might be considered safe, as safety goes in a mine, though there is no such thing as absolute safety in any colliery."

On April 30 the coroner's inquest was still in progress. The testimony was simply corroborative, as the other witnesses published. Following is the important evidence that was elicited during this day's testimony.

Joseph Beddal sworn; "I am an inspector of the mines for the Girard heirs, I have visited the mine once or twice a month. The condition of the colliery was about the same as those that had been worked for the same time, there was some undue robbing in some parts along No. 2 level between breasts 11 and 50, over a distance of about three hundred yards, I did not stop the work but made a report of it to the employers, I considered it an unsafe condition. It was squeezing pretty bad on No. 2 level, the pillars were on the move, but could not tell the extent of the workings above. I think I told some of the miners that the mine was working badly, but they said they were used to it and didn't mind. The colliery had been worked for about nineteen years and I thought it had been robbed too closely at this point. I judged it only a matter of time until a general squeeze would occur. Had I been the inside boss I don't think I would have allowed the men to work in No. 2 level, considering the condition of the colliery."

John McIntyre, a miner testified that he worked in the No. 2 Cuyler colliery and had worked in the breast on Saturday before the accident. "I left about one o'clock, the mine was in pretty bad condition when I was working. I went to work on Monday morning

but my 'butty' was not on hand, the boss told me to go to work, I
did so and heard the general order of Mr. Edgar not to go to work.
I sat at the mouth of the gangway for an hour when McLaughlin
came along with his mules, my butty didn't come and I went home.
If he had come I would have went to work. I have been mining
for two years, and supposed there would be a great deal of noise
before the fall occurred, the pillars were 'Chipping' some every day,
but we didn't mind it, I would not have gone down to timber if I
had known the place was working."

Henry Joyce, a miner also testified that he worked in No. 4 level
and worked the Saturday before the accident. "I told some of the
men I met that there would be a 'mess' there some day. 'Chipping'
has been going on for several months, my breast was west of the fall.
Michael Purcell, brother of Nick Purcell, one of the accident victims
testified that he did not think the condition of the mine was any
worse than it was before, I always felt a little afraid of the place."

On Monday May 4th, the body of Michael Harritty, one of the
miners who worked in the No. 4 lift was exhumed from the mine.
His body was in the same condition as the others found, being in
an advanced state of decomposition, and scarcely recognizable. His
funeral took place on May 5th in the afternoon.

The coroner's inquest would find the probable cause of this accident to be
a fall of a large area of overlying strata.

THE NANTICOKE NO. 1 SLOPE "A DEADLY RUSH OF WATER AND QUICKSAND"

NANTICOKE, PENNSYLVANIA

DECEMBER 18, 1885

Accidents due to flooding cannot always be helped. Abandoned workings will fill with water and muck. An accidental firing of a shot or the simple blow of a pick on the face could weaken the barrier pillar separating a flooded area from a working area and cause a major inrush of water to sweep into the lower workings with irresistible force, killing any miner or laborer in its path and occasionally resulting in total destruction of the working area. In the Susquehanna Basin in the Wyoming Valley of northeastern Pennsylvania much difficulty has been encountered while mining through the quicksand deposits in the area. An ever-present danger surrounded the men who worked in the Nanticoke No. 1 Slope, owned and operated by the Susquehanna Coal Company. At about ten o'clock on Friday morning, December 18, 1885, in the Ross vein a sudden and very unexpected large body of wet quicksand, so saturated by water that it flowed like a liquid, broke into the main gangway, trapped and killed twenty-six men and boys before they had time to react and escape.

THE NANTICOKE NO. 1 SLOPE
"A DEADLY RUSH OF WATER AND QUICKSAND"

Colliery, Showing Shaft and Breaker, Nanticoke, Pa.

A view of the Nanticoke Colliery, Nanticoke, Pennsylvania. *Courtesy of the author.*

The men went off to work at the No. 1 Slope as usual, arriving at the mine about 7:00 a.m. The men and boys descended into the slope. Mine Foreman Mike Corgan was in the mine and walked up the gangway to the face where Abram Lewis and Ed Mathews were working and talked to them. He then went on his inspection. On his way out he saw the young driver boys coming in with their mules and empty cars. Nothing seemed abnormal.

Johnny Zeperko, a Polish miner, was working up in the fourth counter and was the first to see the flood coming. About an hour before the flood, Zeperko noticed that two collars were broken and more water than usual was coming in. Then at 10:00 a.m., while he climbed down into the gangway he heard the water rushing toward him. He shouted to the others to get out. He only saved himself by a heroic effort of wading and swimming a long distance with the inrushing water. Zeperko saw some of his comrades up to their shoulders, struggling for life in the fast-moving swirling water. He finally waded and got ahead of the water, alarming all who he could see. With all possible speed the men in this area ran for their lives and were saved.

This accident was one of the most unforgettable mining disasters that ever affected the families and miners of the region. For up to four days families and friends were led to believe that their loved ones were in an area where they were safe from the quicksand and would be rescued. Upon finding the exact location of the cave-in all hopes were instantly gone when it was discovered that no one could have survived. This is the story of that terrible

Miner loading coal at the face. *Courtesy of the Historical Society of Schuylkill County.*

Here two miners and a driver boy pose with their "Sweetheart of the Mines," their mule. *Courtesy of the author.*

disaster and how hourly reports went from hope and optimism to despair and dread. This is how it was reported by the *Pottsville Miners Journal*.

The news was first reported on December 18, 1885, in the Saturday issue of the newspaper. The headings read:

> An exciting mine disaster—A thousand miners flying for life—The Nanticoke Shaft suddenly flooded—The frightened men driven to the Bottom—All but thirty Rescued—Hopes of saving all
> Nanticoke was thrown into terrible consternation at 11 o'clock this morning by a report that the mines of the Susquehanna Coal

THE NANTICOKE NO. 1 SLOPE
"A DEADLY RUSH OF WATER AND QUICKSAND"

Company were being flooded by water from the river, and that several lives had been lost. The break was in the No. 1 slope, and the volume of water pouring in was so great, that before the miners and laborers could get away from the breasts in which they were working the water was more than a foot deep on the gangway and rising rapidly. Tools were abandoned, driver boys left their mules in the gangway, and all fled for points of safety. Before the workmen were all out the water was breast high. Several men are reported missing, and it's feared they have been drowned. As soon as messengers could be dispatched an alarm was spread to the other workings, Nos. 1 and 2 shafts and No. 2 slope, all of which are connected with the slope and are of lower and greater depth. The alarm was promptly acted upon and the workmen summoned to the foot of the shafts and hoisted ten at a time to the surface. The coal begrimed faces denoted great fear for the safety of their fellows below, and they waited anxiously around the mouth of the shaft until the last workman known to be in the mines was out.

Wives and children gathered in great numbers, full of anxiety for their husbands and fathers, and gladly did they welcome them when they were brought to the surface. One slope is four hundred feet deep, while adjoining shafts and connecting mines are from 600 to 1,600 feet deep. The water continues to flow in in large quantities, but it is not positively known whether it comes from the creek or the river. Until its whereabouts is discovered no definite plans for checking the flooding can be determined. Superintendent Morning is personally looking after matters, and as quickly as possible he will set the pumps at work to clear the mines. The workings now affected by the inflow employ upwards of fifteen hundred men and boys, all of whom will be thrown out of employment for sometime. The mines of the Susquehanna Coal Company are under the control of the Pennsylvania Railroad, and work steady.

The missing men at No. 1 slope are Polanders, who if they did escape, were so much alarmed that through their ignorance they failed to report to the mining boss. The damage done will be considerable, and unless the inlet through which the water finds its way into the slope is discovered, the mines will soon be completely flooded, in which case it would require several weeks to remove the water and get back to working order.

DEATH IN THE MINES

OVER THIRTY MEN MISSING

This afternoon the excitement over the flooding of the No. 1 slope has reached a high point over the report that upwards of thirty men employed on rock work and a half dozen slope men are imprisoned in an old working, the mouth of which is closed by mine timbers and broken cars that were forced against it by the rushing waters. The only means of exit now from the slope is through the air shaft.

Through this space twenty-nine men and boys were rescued by means of a rope, which were lowered and fastened about their bodies, and one at a time they were drawn to the surface. As each one was safely landed terrific shouts of rejoicing arose from the hundreds of people present. It is now supposed that the water that is rushing in comes from the creek not the river.

Everything in the track of the flood was swept before it, the men being knocked about promiscuously and in all cases they report miraculous escapes. The experience of old miners who were caught by the flood say it was the most terrible they ever passed through.

The names of the imprisoned miners, laborers and boys still in the abandoned breast at the slope are: Oliver, Will and Frank Kilver, brothers, miners; Thomas Clifford, doorboy; Willis Dahaney, driver; William Elkie, driver; Lewis Turbey, company man; Isaac Sarber, laborer; Harry Dowe, miner; John Shutt, miner; John Hawk, laborer; John Barber, laborer; August Mital, miner; and several others whose names cannot be learned. The effort of saving these has been started upon, the first rescuing party consisting of inside boss Reese, Mine Boss Corgan, Patrick Doherty, John McKee, John McHalle, Michael Clifford and Thomas Jones having entered the mine. The only danger which is feared for the imprisoned men is from black damp gas which is rapidly accumulating and which the fan can not drive out, owing to the airways being closed up. The disaster is now believed to have been caused by the caving in of a large swamp, covering several acres, upon which culm was being dumped, the accumulating weight of which is supposed to have forced the bottom out.

STILL IMPRISONED

Wilkes-Barre, Dec. 18—Later advices from Nanticoke state that the men employed on rock work in No. 1 slope are reported to have been imprisoned in the upper lifts by the rapid rising of the water. Several miners entered the slope at 3 o'clock with boats and will use every means to reach the men. There is considerable excitement among those at the mouth of the slope, who are anxiously awaiting the return of the rescuing party.

Fully Thirty Men in the Slope

Wilkes-Barre, Dec. 18—At 10 o'clock this evening it is believed that there are fully thirty men in the slope, but no other names can be given. The company is making every possible effort to reach the imprisoned men. The pumps are now at work and new ones are being put up. Another force of men have been sent down the air shaft, who will endeavor to cut through to the spot where the imprisoned men are believed to be. This work will be kept up night and day until the fate of the men is known.

Hopes of Rescuing All

Wilkes-Barre, Dec. 18—The disaster at Nanticoke is more appalling than was first reported. The theory that the water broke through the bed of the river has been dispelled by the fact that the place where the water came in is over 4,000 feet from the Susquehanna. In tracing the water it was discovered it came from a possible pool on the surface in which it accumulated from several springs near by. The water had overflowed the rock to a fault in the seam, which was the first outlet for it. It then ran into the gangway and slopes and thence to the lower working of the No. 1 slope. When the water was discovered rushing into the slope, there were nearly one thousand men and boys at work in the various openings, but at the particular spot whence the water first appeared, there were not over thirty persons at work at one time. It is now reported that there are about twenty men in the face of the gangways who are shut in by the water and rubbish that have accumulated in the west gangway of the second lift of the Ross seam. It is impossible to say what their fate will be. Rescuing parties are now following the face of the chambers of that part of the gangway which is filled with water and rubbish with the hopes of reaching the men sometime during the night. The officials say there is no danger of the men suffocating as they will get plenty of air from the fans of the chambers that are not filled with water and rubbish. The pumps will be put into operation this evening. They have a capacity of removing two thousand gallons of water per minute, and it is expected the mine will be clear by Monday next. Old miners are of the opinion that the men who are shut up will be rescued alive.

More Cheering News

Wilkes-Barre, Dec. 18—Information received here at 11:30 P.M. from Nanticoke gives more cheering news. The water has subsided and a large force of men are at work removing the quicksand that blocks the gangways. The rescuing party are now within forty feet of the men and there are strong hopes of reaching them by morning in time to save their lives. The damage to the mine will be great and it will be some weeks before work can be resumed in the No. 1 slope.

The next reports were published in the Monday issue of the *Evening Journal*:

The Nanticoke Mine Catastrophe
Entombed Miners Not Yet Reached
Rescuers Working Under Great Difficulties

Wilkes-Barre, Dec. 20—To-day was the gloomiest Sunday ever witnessed in Nanticoke. Thousands of people poured into the town in vehicles, on horseback, and afoot. Hundreds of them gathered in groups around the various workings where they discussed the situation of the men imprisoned in the flooded mine. A message was brought here from Nanticoke this morning to the effect that the body of William Eik had been found in the gangway. He had evidently been dead several hours. The officials at the Company's office deny any body has yet been met with. They state that the situation remains unchanged from that of yesterday, though they hourly expect to reach the fatal spot where the entombed men are supposed to be. The rescuing parties are at work continually under the direction of Superintendent Morgan. No hope is now entertained of rescuing any of the victims alive. No. 1 slope where the accident occurred employs about 600 men and boys. Its output is the lowest of any of the Susquehanna Coal Company's operations

A breaker crew poses for this photograph along with the slate pickers, also known as breaker boys, young boys who worked in the dark and dust of a coal breaker sifting through the flowing coal for rock, slate and any impurities. *Courtesy of the author.*

being about 650 car loads a day. The loss to the company will be large, and the next three months will be consumed in making repairs. During that time the men and boys will remain idle, but will be given work at other collieries of the company.

THE WORKING FORCE INCREASED

Wilkes-Barre, Dec. 20—At eight o'clock this evening the rescuing party struck a mass of wet sand and forty five additional men were sent in to remove it with buckets as fast as it was thrown out. At nine o'clock, an official report was received at the company's office here to the effect that the rescuing party was within twenty feet of the fatal chamber, and were hoping to reach the imprisoned men by eleven o'clock.

At 10 o'clock a messenger from the pit in which the relief party are at work, reported to the General Superintendent Stearns that the men were still working vigorously, but had not yet reached the imprisoned miners. From the present outlook it is doubtful they will gain entrance to the fatal slope chamber before tomorrow. Almost as fast as the sand is removed it fills in again, and the men are now laboring under great difficulties.

DEATH IN THE MINES

Wilkes-Barre, Dec 21—At 1:30 o'clock A.M. a report from Nanticoke says that the rescuers have finally reached the place where the men were supposed to be, but they were not there. The rescuing party are now pushing forward to another chamber, with the hopes of finding them in a few hours.

The December 22, 1885 *Evening Journal* reported:

No Cheering Word From Nanticoke
Work Interrupted by a Fall of Earth
Poor Hopes Of Rescuing The Entombed Men

Wilkes-Barre, Dec. 21—At the fatal shaft in Nanticoke this evening little was to be observed of a different nature than what has occurred on other days since the disaster took place. Nanticoke has hitherto been one of the liveliest towns in the coal region, but for the past three days it has been very dull there, as far as coal operations are concerned. At Morgantown, a mining village a few miles from Nanticoke, all the miners suspended work to-day and joined the relief party at Nanticoke. Forty men are now at work at the No. 1 slope which enters the fatal chamber, working on eight hour shifts. One hundred men are vigorously digging away at the air shaft, being relieved every six hours. It is in reaching the imprisoned men by this way that the only hopes are entertained of saving them. Fifty cars of rock and sand are sent out every eight hours from the slope, but the treacherous quicksand mixed with culm, keeps pouring in so that it is impossible to form an idea of the vastness of the work that lies before the relief party. The fan is kept running night and day, but experienced mine bosses doubt whether there is sufficient power to cause fresh air to penetrate the vast obstructions filling the gangway of No. 1 slope. In case the air is cut off the imprisoned men are lost. It is estimated by some persons that the relief party will be able to reach the missing men sometime during the night, but old and experienced miners and mine contractors are of the opinion that it will take at least two days to cut through the barrier.

The Work Interrupted by a Fall

Wilkes-Barre, Dec. 21—About 9 o'clock this evening, the work of the rescuing party was suddenly interrupted by another fall of

116

sand, rock and culm. The men were working on a steep incline, when a vast mass of debris came crashing down toward them with great violence. They fled for their lives and although they escaped uninjured several of them had very narrow escapes. The work of digging for the imprisoned men is for the time suspended, but the officials in charge are making strenuous efforts to overcome the difficulties and continue their labors. They hope to have matters so arranged in an hour or two that work may be proceeded with.

The Last Hope Sinking

Wilkes-Barre, Dec 21—The fall of sand and culm at No. 1 slope in Nanticoke this evening did not come from the surface as was feared at first, but from an upper chamber. The officials in charge after exploration thought it could be overcome in a few hours and at 10:20 P.M. a new gang of ninety men were preparing to go down. Three men, James Turner, John Absalom and Joseph Warren, were caught in the fall, though not badly injured. They were extricated with great difficulty. The men who were at work are now afraid to reenter the mine, and there now appears to be no possible hope of rescuing the imprisoned men alive. They have been imprisoned since Friday morning and even though they may have lived for a time in the breast works they must now die of starvation, if from no other cause. It is believed that it will take several days to penetrate the mass of earth now obstructing the slope.

As day after day passed, hope of rescuing the trapped miners was fading fast. The newspapers continued to follow the story. The *Evening Journal* of December 23 stated:

The Nanticoke Catastrophe—Sad Scenes in the Stricken Town—All Hope of Rescuing the Miners Alive Abandoned—Grief and Despair of the Families—Shafting Proposed, But the Idea Relinquished

Wilkes-Barre, Dec. 22—There was no rest for Nanticoke last night. It is impossible to describe in words the consternation, the dismay and agony which spread through the village when it was learned after midnight that all efforts to get the men out alive were abandoned. The town never saw such a sight as that witnessed from 2 o'clock to 4 o'clock this morning. No one thought of rest.

DEATH IN THE MINES

The whole population was out in the streets discussing in the wildest manner the decision and exclamations of despair, cries of agony, and mutterings of discontent were heard on every street corner and in almost every household. Relatives of the victims were in the wildest agony of despair. Several were seized with convulsions. Fannie Sarver, sister of the two Sarver brothers, was prostrated with violent fits, and at 5 o'clock this morning it was feared would die. Mrs. Kiveler, the old mother of the three Kiveler brothers, was at death's door from weakness and shock, and many other relatives and friends of the victims were completely prostrated. The officials in charge of the rescue work were forced to abandon all work from the air shaft by several irresistible conclusions. Investigations at an early hour this morning show that sand, rock, and culm had fallen to such an extent that the mine in which the imprisoned miners were confined was now filled to the roof, and that the men are dead and beyond all human help. A second cave in took place during the night, which was of very large proportions, and the real extent of the damage done can hardly be guessed, but it is great. This fall brought with it volumes of black damp and sulphurous gases, which has filled the mine and put peremptory stop to all work. At 6 o'clock this morning it was learned that the bodies of the victims cannot be recovered for at least a month, and since this news has spread throughout the mining region the most intense excitement has prevailed. Every effort will now be made to work towards the men from the slope. The clearing up gangways will be pushed as rapidly as possible though the work will be long and tedious, as there is about 3,000 feet of gangway also filled up and said to be packed to the roof.

A Correct List of the Victims

Following is a complete and correct list of the victims as obtained for the first time since the calamity took place.

1. Thomas Clifford, door boy, 14 years
2. William Danahay (Delaney), driver boy, 14 years
3. William Elkie, runner, 19
4. Edward Hargraves, miner, 21, single
5. John Hawk, laborer, 30, single
6. Wadislaus Jeloshinski, laborer, 24, single
7. Oliver Kivler (Kiveler), miner, 27, married, three children

8. William Kivler (Kiveler), laborer, 18
9. Frank Kivler (Kiveler), miner, 32, married, three children
10. Max Longoski, driver, 16
11. Abram Lewis, miner 35, married, three children
12. Andrew Low, miner, 26, single
13. Vincent Like, miner, 23, single
14. Edward Matthews, laborer, 20, single
15. August Matule, miner, 26, single
16. Peter Motulewick, laborer, 25, single
17. Joseph McCarthy, miner, 25, married
18. John Norwack, miner, 26, single
19. Adam Rubinski, laborer, 27, married, two children
20. Isaac Sarver, miner, 26, single
21. John Sarver, laborer, 20, single
22. John Shutt, miner, 28, married, three children
23. Thomas Williams, laborer, 22, single
24. John Drajna, miner, 35, married, three children
25. Michael Adomchick, laborer, 24, single
26. John Sloff, laborer, 27, married, two children

A Shaft to Be Sunk to Reach the Victims

Wilkes-Barre, Dec. 22—The officials of the Susquehanna Coal Company held a meeting this afternoon, and decided to sink a shaft as nearly as possible over the spot where the bodies of the victims lie. The fate of the men in the slope is sealed, and the only thing that remains is to recover the bodies of the victims and restore them to their families and friends. Little has been done to-day except to clear away the debris preparatory to beginning a new shaft and render the machinery and appliances more substantial. The operation at the slope will be kept up and all the debris removed as fast as possible. The most practical miners are of the opinion that when the dead men are found it will be in their chambers. If they have been caught in the fall of sand and culm then the victims will be found one by one as the excavation continues, and it may be two months before the last body is recovered. The loss to the company is estimated this afternoon at $150,000 and will be greater in the cost of sinking a shaft, loss time, and the clearing away of a mile of debris, sand and rock, which is wedged in a solid mass in the gangway.

Michael Sarver, father of the two Sarver brothers, was among the last who came out of the shaft this morning. He wept like a child. He is very old, and a life long toiler in the mines. In spite of his age he is strong and rugged as ever, and insists upon working every moment that the officials will allow him. He expressed himself today as entirely satisfied with the work being done to extricate the men. He did not place any blame for the disaster upon anyone holding that it was entirely accidental. "I have two as fine sons as ever a father had lying down there," he said, "and as good a daughter as a man could wish lying dead at home; but it is the will of God, and I say His will be done. It is a terrible affair, and others are suffering as much as I am. I will go down again as soon as they let me, and I will work day and night to rescue them, dead or alive."

The Shaft Project Abandoned

Wilkes-Barre, Dec. 22—The project of sinking a shaft over the workings of the fatal slope at Nanticoke has been abandoned. It is said it would be necessary to go down 250 feet to reach the nearest gangway and to do so would take three months or more. The company will continue work clearing the obstructed tunnel in hope of gaining entrance to the fatal chamber within the next ten days.

This was the last of the news reports regarding the Nanticoke accident carried in the *Pottsville Evening Journal*. The company kept up the operation and the promise of retrieving the bodies of the entombed men and boys. Working for over four months, miners and laborers reopened the gangway a distance of more than two thousand feet, but not one body was recovered. By the end of April, the officials of the Susquehanna Coal Company were afraid to continue risking the lives of the miners working on the rescue effort. On April 21, 1886, they ended the recovery effort. It was the company's opinion that the bodies could not be reached and that the lives of the workmen would be jeopardized to an unwarrantable extent.

It is interesting to note that after 1846, when six miners were unable to be found in a cave in Carbondale, all bodies of the victims of mine accidents had been restored to their families and friends up until this accident in 1885. In some cases it was done at great expense to the companies involved.

By July 1886 it was noted that nothing like this accident had ever occurred in the region, an accident of such great calamity it has pained everyone connected with the mining of coal.

✝

EPILOGUE

While growing up in the hard coal region of Pennsylvania, I was always aware of the danger associated with working in the mines. Many times I heard the different stories about relatives who were killed or severely injured in mining accidents. It wasn't until I began research on this book that I was struck by the extreme danger of working in the mines and the toll this dangerous work exacted on many families throughout northeastern Pennsylvania. Everyday we turn on our electric lights, utilize our computers, watch our TVs, all with little or no awareness of the source of energy that powers them. For several centuries and even today, coal was a major source for meeting our energy needs. I doubt many ever realize the price paid by miners so that we can have our everyday comforts. We know so little about miners and how much they have sacrificed for us.

In general, coal mining in the United States is much safer than in the past, but still mining accidents happen. Tragically, nineteen miners were killed in the first five weeks of 2006. As usually happens after a disaster, government officials moved quickly. In Pennsylvania, the governor ordered a safety inspection of all seventy-seven current active underground mines. Following the recent accident at the Sago Coal Mine in West Virginia, Congress enacted a hearing to discuss coal mine safety.

It is interesting to see how the media of the nineteenth and early twentieth centuries utilized the local newspapers to alert the public about mining disasters. At the accident site, the reporters graphically recorded what they saw and in turn shared their impressions with their readers. They did not intrude on the privacy of the families and seemed to have empathy for them. They certainly were not sensitive to issues of ethnic diversity, but they allowed a certain respect to exist between the reporting of the sad news and feelings

EPILOGUE

of the families. Today when an accident occurs, the media will move cameras, reporters, radio and satellite transmitters to the site. They bleatingly intrude on the families' privacy for months of media frenzy, including watching the reactions of the grieving families, wanting to know who mined the coal, why they mined the coal and the crazy stories of what can happen while mining coal. Their selfish aim is all for a story and ratings that will soon be forgotten shortly after the last body is brought to the surface.

I recently saw a documentary on television stating that the most dangerous job in the United States is crab fishing in Alaska. When I give tours over four hundred feet below the surface in the dark, damp, cramped confines of the Pioneer Tunnel Coal Mine at Ashland, Pennsylvania, I take exception to the documentary's claim. I explain the difference between the two occupations in terms of the years of working in deep mines, the difficulty of the work conditions and how hard the work is. I tell visitors the number of men killed over the years in the mines and the long-term effects on the men's health. I ask the tourists if they still think crab fishing is the most dangerous occupation in the world.

Based on total numbers killed and injured, coal mining is the most dangerous occupation in the United States. As long as there is coal mining it will continue to be the most dangerous occupation in the United States. According to the Department of Labor thirty out of one hundred thousand miners working in the country die each year in mining-related accidents. And this trend continues into the twenty-first century. As of September 2006 thirty miners had been killed in underground accidents and eight were killed while working on the surface at mining facilities. While working underground, seventeen miners had been killed in explosions of gases or coal dust, six in falls off roofs, two by machinery, three by haulage methods and two by fire in the mines. These are the same types of accidents that have plagued the industry from its inception.

Reflecting on these statistics, it is interesting to note that in 1922, three thousand men were killed in the mines and over two hundred thousand were injured. The *Miners' Safety Almanac* for 1922 stated that more than half of these deaths and injuries were caused by the carelessness of those killed and injured or by the carelessness of a fellow employee. Today, many accidents happen in the same way. But as long as there is coal mining there will always be roof falls, explosions of gas and haulage accidents. Companies will take shortcuts to save money. Miners will do dangerous things. No man in his right mind will deliberately do something dangerous, but it is said that "familiarity breeds contempt" and in no occupation is this saying truer than mining. Men

EPILOGUE

will face dangerous conditions day after day without being killed or getting hurt and they gradually come to think that they are immune to danger. It is then that the chances of injury increase many fold.

While studying these mining accidents of the past, we are aware of the dangers that were evident in this most dangerous of all occupations. This danger still exists today. The smaller number of fatalities today is due to the far fewer miners working in the mines. In truth, as we move into the twenty-first century and we as a nation look for alternate fuel sources, we must be aware that there are more than seventy-six billion tons of coal remaining in Pennsylvania alone, twelve billion in anthracite and sixty-four billion in bituminous. If we eventually mine this coal, we can expect an increase in the number of deaths and injuries associated with coal mining. Because of recent relaxations of health and safety regulations and slashing of budgets for safety inspections, all our future and current miners, unfortunately, will be exposed to continuing danger. Mining, once deadly, will continue to extract its high cost in terms of human lives.

ALSO FROM THE HISTORY PRESS

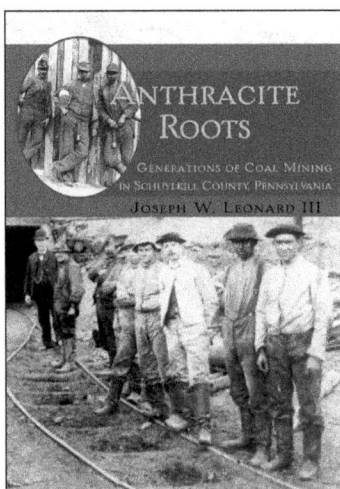

ANTHRACITE ROOTS
Generations of Coal Mining in Schuylkill County, Pennsylvania
Joseph W. Leonard III
978-1-59629-050-1 • $16.99

In this stirring account, author and former coal miner Joseph W. Leonard III provides a means for understanding and fully appreciating the crucial work the brave men of the anthracite mines have done throughout the years. The mining tradition in Leonard's family spans five generations in Schuylkill County, and his family's stories illustrate with touching candor the plight of many thousands of Coal Belt families who stood proud through years of watching their sons, fathers and husbands descend down the shafts into darkness.

Leonard recalls with stunning detail the unforgiving conditions—cave-ins, explosions and choking dust—that he and his forebears endured in the mines. Also captured are poignant tales of the kindness and compassion that permeated mining communities in the face of so much hardship. The intense struggles and quiet successes in *Anthracite Roots* are a testament to the unsung heroes of America's coal mines and the work they have done to power a nation.

Complete with more than forty photos.

Visit us at
www.historypress.net

www.ingramcontent.com/pod-product-compliance
Lightning Source LLC
Chambersburg PA
CBHW060808100426
42813CB00004B/994